A BOOK OF MEDITATIONS

SIMPLE
WONDERS

Other books by Christopher de Vinck

The Power of the Powerless
Only the Heart Knows How to Find Them
Songs of Innocence and Experience
Augusta and Trab

A BOOK OF MEDITATIONS

SIMPLE WONDERS

THE DISARMING PLEASURE OF LOOKING BEYOND THE SEEN

CHRISTOPHER DE VINCK

ZondervanPublishingHouse
Grand Rapids, Michigan

A Division of HarperCollins*Publishers*

Simple Wonders
Copyright © 1995 by *Christopher de Vinck*

Requests for information should be addressed to:

ZondervanPublishingHouse
Grand Rapids, Michigan 49530

Library of Congress Cataloging-in-Publication Data

de Vinck, Christopher, 1951–
    Simple wonders : the disarming pleasure of looking beyond the seen / Christopher de Vinck.
      p. cm.
    ISBN: 0–310–49891–0
    1. Spiritual life—Meditations. 2. Devotional calendars.   I. Title.
BV4811.D46 1995
242–dc 20

                                      95–12497
                                         CIP

International Trade Paper Edition ISBN: 0–310–20406–2

This edition printed on acid-free paper and meets the American National Standards Institute
Z39.48 standard.

Edited by Mary McCormick and John Sloan
Interior design by Sue Koppenol

Printed in the United States of America

95 96 97 98 99 00 01 02 /❖ DC/ 10 9 8 7 6 5 4 3 2

To Fred Rogers and
his neighborhood

Contents

Acknowledgments

I would like to thank John Sloan for his help and care in the formation of this book. If it were not for John, *Simple Wonders* would never have been written. I would also like to thank Mary McCormick for her superb editing and her unwavering support and kindness.

Stop and consider God's wonders.

JOB 37:14

Introduction

He searches the source of the rivers and brings hidden things to light.

JOB 28:11

When I was a high school student, my teachers of English tried to explain the meaning and value of poetry. No matter what poem we read in class, I always had the same comment: "If Robert Frost wants to say something about fences, why doesn't he just come right out and say it instead of talking about neighbors and good relationships?"

Robert Frost, Carl Sandburg, Emily Dickinson all said things in ways that seemed confusing and roundabout. "Get to the point!" I would say in my adolescent whisper.

When I was a teenager, poetry was a collection of hidden messages. Now that I look back, much of what it meant to be young seemed to depend upon mystery and on the unavoidable circumstance of being ignorant. I just did not see things the way that other people did. I would look at a painting and see a horse with some old guy leaning against a lance. I would listen to a classical piece of music and hear just a bunch of toots and violins.

Youth skates on the surface of the ice; but then, as we grow older, a bell rings, or a word is said, or a particular color is illuminated, and slowly there is the realization that there is something more.

I remember kneeling one winter on the ice of the swamp beyond the woods of my house. My sister zoomed ahead of me. Johnny, my neighbor and best friend, chased after Anne. I leaned over the ice and began swirling my glove on the ice's surface. At first I saw a faint orange color, and then I saw a goldfish looking up at me through the ice.

"Hey, you guys! There's a fish under here!"

"What did you expect to see?" Johnny said with laughter. "An elephant?"

I never thought about the fish in winter. Something was down there, under the surface, still swimming around.

When I read for the first time John Steinbeck's novel *The Grapes of Wrath*, I saw and felt things I had never seen or felt before. The people in that book were in great pain, and I suffered with them. I never felt these things before about a book.

I knew that I wanted to become a writer when I read the poetry of William Carlos Williams. He wrote about old men, young men, old women, and young women. He sang about trees and grass and children with twirling toys. He was able to write about a funeral, about a woman giving birth, about a man dancing in his room, in ways that made me understand things under the surface of the ice. Williams taught me how to write in the language of an ordinary person saying ordinary things. The writer's magic, however, is in the ability to identify the ordinary in the name of beauty, or passion, or loneliness, or God.

This book is a collection of ordinary moments in a single life written in the name of beauty, passion, loneliness, and in the name of God. Each moment is introduced with a few lines from the Bible.

The Bible is a collection of words that say more than the words themselves. Much of the Bible is about ordinary events in life, but in the telling of these events there is the whisper of God, the certitude of salvation, the celebration of light and Christ, so the words take on a different meaning. This is what my English teachers were trying to tell me when I read poetry for the first time.

In the Psalms it is written: "O my people, hear my teaching; listen to the words of my mouth. I will open my mouth in parables, I will utter hidden things, things from of old—what we have heard and known, what our fathers have told us" (Psalm 78:1–3).

This book is a collection of parables, little stories that speak about things that I have seen and felt, but in the telling I have tried to write close to the heart and reveal hidden things that we all feel—innumerable things both small and great placed in an ordinary voice, in the ordinary day.

What I hope you do with this book is to look at the stories and see how they speak to your heart. I would like you to stop skating for a second and kneel down beside me. Here, like this. Now take your glove and swirl it on the ice. Careful—look down through the ice and take a good look. See the fish? Under the surface the fish are swimming.

He gives wisdom to the wise and knowledge to the discerning. He reveals deep and hidden things.

DANIEL 2:21–22

15

God in Surprising Places

Surely the LORD is in this place, and I was not aware of it.
GENESIS 28:16

I met an old woman in a nursing home many years ago when I was in high school. My class was supposed to write a paper about someone over seventy. I didn't know anyone over seventy except for my grandparents, but they were living in Belgium. Then I thought: *I'll visit a nursing home and ask permission to meet someone for my English assignment.*

When I entered the brick building, I walked up to the front desk. A kind woman with glasses sent me to the director's office.

After I explained my assignment to the director, she sent me to room six.

Room six had a bed, a single chair, a desk, and a single picture of a rose on the wall. Sitting in the chair was Mrs. Murphy. She was bent over, knitting diligently. Her needles clicked and ticked. When I knocked on her door, Mrs. Murphy looked up from her knitting and squinted.

"Yes?" she asked.

"I'm from the high school. I'm supposed to write an essay about someone over seventy."

"Step out of the hall light. Come in. Come in." Mrs. Murphy stopped knitting and patted the bed beside her. "Sit here."

I slowly entered the room, which smelled like lemon candy. I sat on the left back corner of the little bed.

Mrs. Murphy returned to her knitting.

"What are you making?" I asked.

"God's in my basket," she answered.

Because I thought that she wasn't very good at hearing, I spoke a bit louder.

"What's in your basket, Mrs. Murphy?"

She stopped knitting again, turned her face in my direction, smiled, and repeated, "God's in my basket."

I looked around the room and finally noticed her knitting basket at the foot of her chair. It was filled with various balls of wool. I leaned forward a little to get a small peek just in case I might catch a glimpse of God.

"Oh, He's there." Mrs. Murphy smiled.

"How can you tell?" I asked.

"I've prayed for Him to come, and He has." With that, Mrs. Murphy returned to her basket and didn't say a word after that. No matter what I asked, she just continued rocking, smiling, and rocking some more.

Finally I stood up, thanked the old woman, and walked back into the bright hall light. Just before I left the building, the director stepped out from another room. She smiled and asked me how things went.

"Not so well," I said with a disappointed edge to my voice. After all, my writing project was a failure. "She thinks that God is in her knitting basket."

"What is your name?" the woman asked.

"Christopher."

"That means *Christ bearer*, doesn't it?" she asked, more as a statement of fact than a question to be verified. "What did you think of Mrs. Murphy?"

"I think she is a little crazy."

"She was when she first arrived," the director said. "When her husband died, she was alone. They didn't have any children. She has no family. She is ninety-three. All she wanted to do was die. That was five years ago. Then she said that all she wanted was peace. I suggested that she pray for peace. So that is what she did. A few months later she discovered knitting. A woman who came to us for a recreation hour taught Mrs. Murphy how to knit. In six months she was knitting socks for everyone. At the Christmas fair she sold over a thousand dollars' worth of socks, wool dolls, sweaters, and blankets. She taught knitting in the local grade school as a volunteer. The children from the school would invite her home for dinner at least three times a week. Mrs. Murphy was the most popular person in our neighborhood and in our nursing home. She was truly happy."

"But what about now?" I asked.

"Well, she no longer remembers very much. She has become so old and sick, she has forgotten everyone's name."

"But she can still knit," I said.

"Yes, Christopher, she can still knit, and she is at peace. And something besides—she says only one sentence."

"God's in her basket."

"Yes, the God of peace."

I never did write my essay for school, but two weeks later a brown package waited for me when I returned home. Inside I found a beautiful, brown wool sweater just my size. I also found a note in a small, white envelope:

Dear Christopher:

Mrs. Murphy asked that we send you this gift. She thought you'd like a bit of God to keep you warm.

Mrs. Murphy died three days ago. She was very happy.

Stop by and visit us again someday.

Sincerely,
Sister Claire Roberts, OFM

How often do you take an active role in seeking out the existence of God? How often do you look around for proof that Christ lived and died for our salvation? Do you ever doubt that God is always beside you? Have no fear. He, our God of peace and mercy, is tugging at your sleeve with His unconditional love.

Lord of the day, keeper of divine secrets, help me see Your face in the faces of those I meet today. Help me recognize Your work in all that I see. I look for Your guidance. I am blessed with the ability to do Your will. In the name of You, Father, I pray for renewed vision so that I may clearly see my way to Your home of peace, to Your house of eternity. In Your name, Father, I pray. Amen.

Touch of God

Father, into your hands I commit my spirit.

During my visit to a second grade classroom in the school district where I work, I asked children what they do when they are sad. Some said that they walk up to their rooms and rest on their beds and think. A boy said that he reads. A girl said that she likes to color when she is sad. Then a boy to my right, sitting in the circle, said, "Well, I pretend that I'm sick."

I didn't understand, so I asked the boy why he did this.

"Well, when I'm sad, I need someone; so if I pretend that I am sick, someone will feel my forehead. I like it when my mother puts her hand on my forehead."

I have been thinking about this answer. A minister friend of mine said that when he visits the hospital, it seems that the best thing he can do is to place his hand on someone's forehead. "People smile almost every time I do this, no matter how ill the person might be."

We live in an age where pills, heating pads, and exercise machines seem to help make us feel better.

Is the hand of another person the hand of healing? When my two sons and my daughter were born, I wanted to kiss the hands of the doctor, the first human hands to hold my children. A farmer runs his hands through the spring soil. A woman combs her hair with her extended fingers.

Often, in the great Russian icons, the image of Christ is holding up His right hand in a blessing. All in the universe stands before the raised hand of God. Perhaps the warm sun upon our bodies is the hand of a healing God.

When I am sad, I often return to my desk and begin to write. The words seem to speak; the words seem to form an image of a person speaking. Often it is my father waving to me across the distance of my own adulthood; often it is the image of my mother. I remember how my mother held a stone on the flat of her palm. She liked to display simple things. "Look at this beautiful stone," she once said. What was beautiful was my mother's hand in the air, stretched out before me.

A few nights ago my daughter Karen had a fever. I placed my hand on her forehead, and she smiled. "Your hand feels so cool. Please leave it there."

God reaches down to us with His hands to soothe our pain. We can feel the power of this healing through the embrace of a neighbor, a doctor, or a loved one. We can sense His touch against our cheeks when we walk out of the house in the morning air. How difficult it is sometimes to offer back to God a human touch upon the face of His infinite glory.

God of all people, I give thanks for the cradle of Your hands. Rock me back and forth today between the moon and sun, protect me today with a single touch of Your fingertip. Trace on my forehead a small cross when I need Your grace. I give thanks to You, my God, for Your touching my life, for being my life. For this I give thanks. Amen.

Delighting in God's Creation

In the beginning God created the heavens and the earth.
GENESIS 1:1

We are odd human beings. We take too much for granted. If we never saw a tree and we suddenly stepped around a corner and saw, for the first time, an oak tree, we would think it was the most extraordinary thing that ever existed.

If we had never seen a jet passenger plane and suddenly a Boeing 747 flew overhead, we would think, perhaps, that a thunder god had zoomed by.

If we never saw a fish, a cat, a car, a strawberry before, how wondrous these things would seem. Unfortunately, the more we are exposed to something, the more and more distance we create between the true marvel and the stale attitude.

People who create a circus try to battle this flaw of ours. They arrange animals in a way that forces us to stop and look closely. An elephant is, well, just an elephant, but make ten elephants march around a circle, or stand on each other's backs, then you have something extraordinary. But can you think of a more extraordinary creature than the elephant? (This is even a wonderful word: *elephant.*)

Shoot a person out of a cannon, and we look closely at a human being. The circus dazzles us with tigers pawing at the trainer, seals climbing ladders, bears dancing. What is left if we take the music away, and the ringmaster, and the clowns, and the costumes?

What is left if we wash the paint off the elephant's hide? What if we take the hat off the bear's head? What is left?—just a bear, just a few elephants, and men and women standing around on the sawdust.

If we can teach ourselves to look closely at the things that surround us, we will be dazzled. A dog, a DOG is an extraordinary creature. Did you ever appreciate a screen in the window? What a wonderful invention. I think a bicycle is one of the most extraordinary inventions—all that spinning and chains and balance and metal. We can travel faster on a bicycle than a running athlete can, and visit anywhere in town without gasoline, money, insurance, or a license.

Do you remember the delight you felt after you created something: a flower arrangement, a painting, a garden, a baby, a report, a song? Can you imagine the delight God must have felt after He created the sun, the moon, the earth and all its treasures? Can you imagine how pleased He was when He created *you*?

God the artist. God the craftsman. God the maker. Walk through the day as if you are visiting an art gallery and take delight in all that you see framed in heaven's gold.

I think God must have had lots of fun when He created carrots.

I am worthy, Lord, of a place beside the redwood trees. I am worthy to stand in the lilies of the field. I am worthy, Lord, to swim with the dolphins, to breathe the mountain air. I am worthy this day to take my place in Your creation. I am worthy, Lord, of Your delight, Master, Carpenter, Builder of stars and hope. I am worthy. Amen.

The Kindness of God

But when the kindness and love of God our Savior appeared, he saved us, not because of righteous things we had done, but because of his mercy.

TITUS 3:4

Josh was the old man next door. He raised his own chickens, sold eggs, planted his own garden, and sold vegetables. I was afraid of Josh when I was a child. He was always stooped over when he walked. He could not speak many words in English. I once saw him chop off the head of one of his chickens. Josh didn't have many teeth.

One early September morning my mother asked me if I would run down to Josh's and buy some tomatoes. My mother wanted to add some flavor to her stew. I had never walked to Josh's house alone before. I was always accompanied by my older brother or sister whenever we were asked to make a purchase down at Josh's place.

Always an obedient boy, I did as my mother asked. My mother handed me a dollar to pay for the tomatoes. After I stood before Josh's house for a long time, I pulled the string of the bell that hung from the front door.

"Yes?" he asked as he opened the door and looked at me.

"My mother would like two tomatoes." I wanted to run.

"In the back." Josh closed the door, and by the time I stepped to the back of his house, he was already there standing beside his vegetable stand. I watched as he reached over with his big hands and lifted four tomatoes and placed them into a brown bag. He reached down and handed me the bag. "No charge." I looked up at him, and he smiled, revealing his few teeth and his good heart.

I never forgot Josh over these thirty years. A little kindness goes a long way.

Sometimes we think that God is a frightening power that oversees all that we do with a gruff cast of His eye. Like a child confronting the strong, old vegetable man, we can sometimes be intimidated by the truth and mystery in God's love for us, but then His infinite kindness is revealed in a minister's words, in an embrace from a parent, in a quiet understanding that our suffering no longer exists.

You are placed in many positions of power: in your home, in your work, in your relationships with strangers. Such power exercised with kindness will earn you not only great respect but will also allow others to see your smile—a human, God-given trait we sometimes forget to exhibit. Perhaps you can extend a kind gesture toward the first person you see today.

I can stand before You, Lord, in meekness, in my fear of You and tremble, but in Your kindness You have said, "Do not be afraid, for I am with you" (Genesis 26:24). In Your kindness I sing. In Your kindness I take comfort. In You, God, I am not afraid. Amen.

Thanksgiving in the Bathroom

Let us come before him with thanksgiving, and extol him with music and song.

PSALM 95:2

Today I clean the bathroom. Whenever I return to this task, I am reminded how stable my life is. To clean the bathroom demands a sense of peace, a place of peace, and a time of peace. I see the history of the world each day in the newspaper: a new battle, a new death caused by carelessness or evil. I am a careful listener, hearing a neighbor's explanation on the new tax-hike, or my sister's recalling a day when she and I ate fresh peppers together at the edge of a distant farm that seemed to never have existed after all.

When I turn the bathtub faucet to the right, clear, cool water gushes out against my hands. In some parts of the world, water is almost as valuable as gold. In some homes in the world, water will determine if the children will live another month.

We who are civilized eat on porcelain plates and bathe in porcelain tubs. I watched a television program showing children bathing in gutter water and using their hands to brush away the dust in the road in search of single grains of rice to chew and swallow for their inflated stomachs.

I like to wash the bathroom floor. The soap foams up, and I take my socks and shoes off, and then I slide around as if I am skating, though I don't tell anyone about this habit. Remember the ancient man found in the frozen tundra? He had a grin of pain etched on his face. Man buried in the ice. Man skating on the ice field of a suburban bathroom.

The toilet is easy to clean because there is a constant source of fresh water to flush down the soap. The kings of the fourteenth century didn't have flush toilets.

The bathroom tiles are the easiest to clean. A simple squirt with the spray bottle and a quick wipe with a sponge, and the tiles shine. Each time I drive to New York City, someone tries to wash my windshield with a spray of water and a quick wipe with a squeegee.

Sometimes when I wash the sink, the cat jumps up and dabs her paw into the water. She sometimes falls in, scrambles out, jumps to the floor, and runs out the door, leaving a trail of water and paw prints on my fresh and clean floor.

Each time I wash the bathroom, I stop for a moment and stare out the skylight above my head. I cannot see much except the sky and the branch of an oak tree. Sometimes a bird flies overhead. In the winter the skylight is covered with snow, but I still look up and admire the underside of winter's blanket spread out upon the house. Lord have mercy.

The last thing I clean when I wash the bathroom is the mirror. I wipe the mirror's surface with a damp sponge, then, with broad strokes, I dry the mirror with a paper towel only to discover myself staring back at me.

Who is that in the mirror? My children call me Daddy. My wife calls me Chris. I consider myself to be a writer, a man full of joys and regrets, a man in the center of the bathroom, smelling the soap, feeling the sunlight against my head, a man in the center of a civilized world, daring to feel intelligent, satisfied, confident in my cleverness; and yet,

I am a man full of weakness, realizing how grateful I ought to be for the peace and privilege to clean the bathroom.

It is easy for me to forget the source of all my happiness. It is easy to forget who gave me the ability to lift my hand and wash the bathroom walls.

I like to look at a map and trace where the great rivers of the world begin, for they all begin with a small stream of water at the top of a mountain that slowly rolls down to join other water and eventually becomes the Mississippi River. How easy it is to forget that God is the source, that God is the water that holds us all together so that we can form the river of life on this earth.

It is easy to overlook His part in our daily work. Too often we believe it is the labor that is at the center of what we do. I believe the cause of that labor ought to drive our work, and I believe all good labor is accomplished in the name of God—even cleaning the bathroom.

Each of our routines can be an act of gratitude to our Lord Jesus Christ, who suffered and died for us so that we can know the true way through our workaday world.

God, trace my hands with Your fingers so that I may be guided in my work today to do Your will. Accept my efforts as a greeting and a sign of my gratitude.

Lord of all labor, I offer my work as a prayer for those who are in pain, God of power and might, God of labor and mercy. Amen.

Hidden Fear

Fear and trembling seized me.

JOB 4:14

When my son Michael was four years old, he returned one afternoon from his friend's house after wading in a small pool for a few hours. As he stepped into the house, he blurted out a new word, a word that wasn't acceptable in our house.

"Where did you learn to say that?" I asked.

Michael looked up at me.

"If you say that word again, I am going to wash your mouth out with soap," I said against my better judgment.

Michael looked up at me and said, simply, "Okay."

I was satisfied that I had made my point and the whole thing was forgotten, or so I thought.

One week later I was in the dining room, helping my older son with a puzzle. I turned when I heard Michael standing in the doorway. There he stood with these huge tears in his eyes. I left the table and walked up to him.

"Michael. What's wrong? Is everything okay?"

"Daddy. I don't want to die," Michael wept with a voice I had never heard him use before, a voice of deep sadness.

"But what do you mean, Michael?" I asked as I embraced him.

"You said you were going to put soap in my mouth." Here Michael simply broke down in a sob. "And if you do, the soap will hurt me and make me die."

For a whole week my little boy had carried this terrible idea in his head and finally he poured out his fear and regret.

I was startled with this child's determined will to live against such a frightful power as soap death.

Have you been carrying a hidden fear for some time? Have you allowed that fear to build up over an extended period of time? Have your hidden fears silenced you, taken you away from an inner peace?

Perhaps you can learn from a four-year-old child's experience: Bring your fears to someone you trust.

God gave us the power to comfort our friends. They are waiting for you with open arms.

For the comfort of Your arms, we thank You, Lord. For the words of Your Son, we praise You. For the comfort of faith, we thank You, Lord. For the gift of grace, we praise You. Amen.

Are There Turtles in Heaven?

Faith is being sure of what we hope for and certain of what we do not see.

HEBREWS 11:1

Do you remember a time in your childhood when you questioned the existence of heaven?

I remember when I was a boy walking through the swamps behind our house along the bank of a narrow, deep canal. Suddenly the still water began to undulate; small waves rippled against the bank. I leaned over and looked into the water. I saw the faint outline of a huge snapping turtle pass before me, then it dived deep into the dark water and disappeared. *Where do turtles go?* I wondered.

"Are there turtles in heaven?" I asked my mother later that day.

"Of course there are. Lots of them."

As I grew older, I continued to ask about the quality of heaven.

"Can I bring my cat, Moses, there?"

"Yes."

"Will I recognize you, Mom?"

"Yes."

"Can we have raspberries in heaven? I like raspberries."

"Yes."

In my early twenties I asked, "With all that we know about science, is heaven perhaps just beyond the expanding universe?"

And now that I am in my forties I have been asking myself a more direct question: "Is there a heaven?" I find myself asking this question more and more because I do not want to leave my wife and children when I someday die. I do not want them to be alone. I want to be with them always.

So this is what I have come to believe: Heaven is a place for cats and turtles, and for my mother and father, and for my wife and children, and for everyone.

My life is connected to an acceptance that some questions can only be answered with one word: faith.

Christ promised us paradise as He was dying on the cross. I believe in that promise. I believe in life everlasting. I believe in God the Father almighty, the Creator of heaven and earth, in all things seen and unseen. I believe. I believe.

Do you?

When I am cold, You provide me with warmth. When I am lonely, You sit beside me and we talk. When I am old, You tell me not to be afraid. Thank You, God, for these examples of Your mercy and generosity. When I fear death, You remind me of salvation. I pray to You, dear God, and give thanks for Your promise that I will someday join You in heaven. Amen.

Breaking Through the Clouds

The sun rises and the sun sets, and hurries back to where it rises.
ECCLESIASTES 1:5

I was reminded of a simple truth while flying home from a recent talk I delivered in Toronto.

I arrived at the airport a bit early, so I sat and read the newspaper about all the gloom and sadness. The gray sky outside was beginning to grow darker. Storm clouds were forming.

After we were allowed to settle inside the plane, after the jet zoomed off heading south, I felt a bit lonely, caught between leaving my new friends and not yet being home with my wife and children.

Something happened. As the Air Canada jet climbed and climbed, I looked out the window into the dark, gray fog that draped itself on the entire country; then, suddenly, the plane broke through the clouds and we were flying under a blue, clean sky with the bronze sun setting in the west.

We can wonder at the meaning of gloomy, rainy days, but we forget that we need the rain to keep the soil rich for our food. God built this house, this universe for us.

No matter how gloomy the day appears, no matter how greatly fog, rain, or snow makes you feel depressed, remember that God is always there behind the curtain, polishing the brass sun.

Today look at one of your troubles and try to see clearly through the fog to that bright, bronze-colored solution.

Open to me, O Lord, a glimpse of Your light. How easily I fall into darkness. How easily I feel the cold. Grant me Your vision, Lord. Let me see beyond what appears as fog, and gloom, and rain. Let me sing to the hidden way. Let me dance toward the dawn's resurrection. Amen.

Safe Haven

When you enter a house, first say, "Peace to this house."

LUKE 10:5

I was sitting on the couch, reading a wonderful book, *Iron and Silk,* by Mark Saltzman. The book is about Mr. Saltzman's two years spent as an English teacher in China. He is a writer with a clear eye for description and a strong heart full of humor and wisdom.

I was reading the section in which some Chinese children were frightened by a ghost story Mark was retelling, when I felt a pressure on my legs, then a full weight of someone crawling up on my chest.

Michael, my young son, had come inside the house after a ride on his bicycle. Without a word, he simply wiggled onto my lap and curled into a comfortable position.

It pleases me greatly that our children feel comfortable enough with my wife and me to simply plop themselves down upon us whenever they feel the need to do so.

It takes a little more rib-cage strength when David, our older son, needs a father or mother pillow.

We all need a safe haven of trust and love to return to after a difficult day at work, or after a tough ride around the neighborhood.

Before Christ was arrested and crucified, He walked to the Mount of Olives. In His fear of the upcoming events, He asked His Father, God almighty, "If you are willing, take this cup from me" (Luke

22:42). Jesus, too, needed a safe haven. Where did He go for protection? It was not a physical place. It was not Mount Olive. In His need for safety, Jesus returned to God, His Father, and then He prayed.

Our true haven is in our prayers to God. We petition the Lord for guidance, for help, for comfort. He is there to do these things. He has promised this to us.

We are reminded each day that God provides His protection for us, just as He sent His confidence and love down to His Son, Jesus Christ.

"Why are you sleeping?" He asked them. "Get up and pray so that you will not fall into temptation." I stand up and pray to the Holy One. I stand up and pray. I am not a person of a lonely distance from You, God, my protector. You are here beside me. Hear my whisper. Here my prayer. Amen, amen, I say to You with gratitude for Your comfort. Amen.

The Good News

Your word, O LORD, is eternal; it stands firm in the heavens. Your faithfulness continues through all generations.

PSALM 119:89–90

When my sister, Maria, was a little girl, I told her "Anthony the Ant" stories, fables I made up about the smallest ant in the world, who was able to accomplish extraordinary feats.

One story described how Anthony carried a whole sugar cube on his back through a terrible rainstorm, which, of course, caused the sugar to melt away.

Another story explained how Anthony fought off a beetle with a sewing needle. I told Maria about Anthony's swinging from cobwebs to rescue his mother from the spider, and about how Anthony was the only creature in the world who could fit through the small hole that led into the giant's cave. (The giant had locked the sun in a wooden chest; Anthony was able to unlock the chest and return the sun to the sky with the help of some butterflies.)

Today Maria is expecting her first child. She and her husband, Peter, have not picked out any names yet. They did not want to have anyone telling them through any special test that the baby is a boy or girl.

All I know for sure about this child is that (1) he or she is very lucky to have Maria and Peter as parents, and (2) I cannot wait for the day when I can whisper into the ear of my niece or nephew: "Once upon a time there was an ant, and his name was Anthony. He was the smallest ant in the world."

Jesus was a storyteller. He explained how we should live through the use of parables. His words of hope and salvation have come down to us through the Bible from generation to generation.

How easy it is to see the delight in a child's face when we tell him or her a favorite fairy tale. Can you imagine the delight in God's heart each time you read His stories in the Bible?

We are blessed year after year, century after century with the Good News.

O Lord, You are not a story; You are not a tale. You are not a fantasy; You are not science fiction. You, Lord God, are truth, all time, all things seen and unseen. I do not guess at Your meaning. I am not confused by Your words. Keep me in Your telling heart. Amen.

The Sheep at the Shepherd's Right

I was a stranger and you invited me in.
MATTHEW 25:35

During our hectic, busy lives we are clearly focused on our responsibilities. We zoom from one schedule to the next to accomplish our tasks. We do not like to be disturbed. We do not like to be slowed down. But Jesus seems to try to divert our attention. He seems to ask us to stop our important work and do some of His important work when we least expect it.

I was driving on Interstate-80 early in the morning, trying to beat the traffic jams, trying to arrive at work early to finish a project. The speedometer read sixty-five miles per hour. I had a full tank of gas. The car was brand-new, shining, sporting a fresh smell and a smooth-running engine.

Suddenly, in the distance I saw, at the side of the highway, a collection of people. The closer I zoomed toward them, the more I realized they had car trouble.

I raced past them, intent on beating the traffic and completing my task at work, but then I looked in the rearview mirror as the people waving their hands grew smaller and smaller. I slowed down, pulled to the side of the highway, and backed up to the stranded people.

It turned out to be what looked like a family: a woman in a dark kerchief, four children sitting on the guardrail, clapping their hands to the beat of a song, and the father standing in front of the open hood of his fifteen-year-old car that obviously wasn't working.

"Do you know car?" the man asked in broken English.

The wife smiled. She was missing many teeth. One of the boys, the older one, stepped up and said with a shy manner, "We are going to visit my uncle. The car stopped. He's getting married this morning."

Married? On a weekday? In the morning? I don't think so. But I did take a look at the old engine. I know absolutely nothing about cars.

"Can you fix?" the father asked. "My brother is married this morning soon."

I looked up and down the empty highway hoping to see a police car, a tow truck, anyone who might be able to help. Then I looked at the family.

"Where is the wedding?"

"Ten miles over the mountain," the wife said with another smile.

I arrived at work four hours late that morning.

"What happened?" my supervisor asked.

"Well, I went to a wedding."

Three weeks later I received in the mail a postcard from the Bahamas from the groom. It read, in part, "Thank you for my brother. His car is good again. My wife, she is going to name our first son 'Christopher.' Good bye."

No work is more valuable than helping a person in need for that person is always Christ, and He will always reward you for your generosity.

I tumble down and I fall. I tumble down and I cry out in pain. I tumble down and I look up for an extended hand, for a soothing voice. Thank You, Lord, for when I am weak, You lift me up and invite me into Your heart, the home of all healing. Amen.

What God Wants You to Do

Your will be done.

MATTHEW 6:10

When I was a high school student, I spent an afternoon with a friend in Canada who ran a bookmobile for the rural poor in the eastern section of Ontario. I rode up front with the young volunteer.

I'll never forget driving in a heavy rainstorm. We drove for twenty minutes until we stumbled upon a farm set down in a bleak valley. My driver friend shifted gears as the truck groaned and slowly shook down this long, mud-filled road toward a small, single house.

As we drove down the hill, I saw to my left a man and two children all bending over the ground, tending to the crops. I didn't know what they were doing in the rain.

My friend in the bookmobile pressed the truck's horn, which sent the children running toward the house. The man stood up straight, placed his hands on his hips, wiped his forehead, then returned to his squatting position and continued working in the field.

A woman greeted us at the door and invited us in.

I had never seen a dirt floor. The two children, a boy and a girl, both under twelve years old, held books in their hands.

"We've done with these," the girl said.

"I'd like another one about hawks," the boy chimed in.

I looked at these children and thought about the carpets in my parent's home, about the books my aunt sent from Belgium that I had never bothered to read.

I became a writer partly because of those two children holding up their books with dirt on their hands, because it was then that I saw the power of the written word.

It seems as if God gives us hints each day about what He'd like us to do. If you look closely around you, or if you listen carefully to what a friend says, I bet you will recognize a potential hint as to what God would like you to do. Perhaps it is as simple of an act as dragging in the neighbor's garbage can, or visiting an old aunt who just says on the phone, "Oh, I'm okay, I guess. It is so cold outside." Perhaps she is really saying, "I'd love a little company today."

Listen carefully. Observe. God is pointing the direction.

Who tells us there is fruit to be plucked from the tree of life? Who tells us there is water to drink from the well of eternity? Who explains there is work to be done in the field of the Lord? You, my God. I listen, and I will act today and all my days for Your will and pleasure. ~

God's Secrets

The secret of the kingdom of God has been given to you. But to those outside everything is said in parables.

MARK 4:11

Early one morning, after struggling to wake up, shower, dress, and slouch toward the orange juice and cereal, I looked out the kitchen window at sunrise, dew, a neighbor's house, forsythia bushes, a robin on the grass. If I had been more awake, I would have realized immediately that robins do not have beards; however, at first I was convinced that this particular robin sprouted a fine, brown beard.

How odd to see something out of the ordinary in the most unlikely places. (I recently read about some college students who dismantled a campus police car and reassembled it on the roof of one of the academic buildings.)

Well, my full consciousness began to spread through my body as I realized, of course, that robins do not have beards but wings . . . red breasts . . . feet . . . eyes. Then I understood that the robin had a mouthful of dried grass.

She's building a nest, I thought.

I learned long ago that if I wait long enough, eventually what I watch will eventually lead me to a conclusion, or to a destination, or to home. Scientists, pilots, and lonely people all recognize this truth.

So I watched the robin peck at the dry grass a bit, pick up a few more thin strands, look to the left, then to the right. (She didn't look in the kitchen.) Then she pushed off and pressed her wings into the air and disappeared instantly in the forsythia bush three feet above where she had originally stood.

That afternoon, after a busy day at work, I parked the car in the driveway, walked up the brick steps into the kitchen. The children greeted me at the door.

"I've got a secret," I announced.

"Are we going to the shore?" Karen asked. She often equates secrets to a surprise trip.

"Are we gonna have pizza?" Michael asked.

My teenage son just rolled his eyes, thinking, *Another of Dad's great secrets.*

"Follow me," I whispered as I stepped out the kitchen and back to the driveway. "Over here. Don't tell anyone."

We gathered before the forsythia, and I pointed to the nest deep within the green bush. "There's a nest," I announced.

David rolled his eyes. Karen was disappointed that we weren't going to the shore, but she was interested in the nest. Michael asked, "Is there an egg?"

I didn't know, so I lifted Michael as he stretched his neck, pulled back a few green branches. "Nope. No eggs." This news convinced Karen that the shore was definitely the better secret. David was already back in the house.

The next morning, after a desperate lunge out of bed, after my shower, after dressing, and eating breakfast, I stumbled through my near sleep and out the back door and began to walk toward the car. Just before I stepped into the car, I had a thought. I walked back up the driveway, walked on the grass, and stood before the forsythia. I reached in, pulled a few branches back, stood on my toes, and peered in. One blue egg.

That night, after work, I entered the kitchen with the newspaper under my arm as the children called out, "Daddy's home!"

As I stooped down among my three children, I whispered, "I've got a secret!"

We have to be open to the hidden things that are placed before us. We need to pay close attention to the gifts that appear in simple disguises.

In this new day remember that you are a child of God standing before His watchful eye. I believe He hopes that you will discover His secrets, as children discover new things each day. Be open to God's gifts. They need to be unwrapped, discovered, and appreciated.

Think how odd it is when Jesus says that the first will be last. There is a secret there. Think about the parable of how the good seeds will grow on good ground. There is a secret there. I believe the secret is the divine gift from God. He is everywhere, hidden in the bud of a spring flower and revealed in splendor in the laughter of your neighbor.

I believe I am a mystery, Lord, closed within my body and heart. I believe this mystery is today's frontier, the place for You, my God, to enter and reveal who I truly am. I take Your hand and dare to step out of my mask and share my faith with those I will greet today in the reality of love.

Drawn Swords

His speech is smooth as butter, yet war is in his heart; his words are more soothing than oil, yet they are drawn swords.

I stood in line at the food market waiting to pay for my loaf of bread and gallon of milk. Over in the next aisle another long line of people waited to pay for their groceries. My eyes wandered from the cashier, to the magazine rack, to the advertisements hanging on the large windows of the store.

Then I happened to watch a woman, perhaps in her fifties, push her cart up to the adjacent cashier and begin to place the items onto the black, rolling conveyor belt.

If you look closely at what goes on around you, you never know what you will learn.

As the cashier struck the cream-colored keys on her machine, adding up the cost for the different items, the customer placed a coupon upon a can of coffee. The food made its way along the conveyor belt.

The customer began to look around for a moment. She stopped pulling the food out of her cart, and she waited. I was curious about what she was, or seemed to be, waiting for.

The cashier reached for the coupon and for the coffee.

"This coupon is outdated," the cashier said in a harsh, triumphant voice.

"Oh, really?" the customer replied, projecting an air of innocence, with a nasty voice of indignation, revealing that she knew all along that the coupon was, indeed, outdated.

I do not fully understand why people are so cruel to each other. I do not fully understand why people try to take, take, take.

How do we expect our world of nations to join hands and celebrate when two women at the checkout line in the corner grocery store battle with sneers on their faces for the right to fifteen cents?

Jesus is our Father. When asked what we ought to do in the world, He said that we should love one another. Each day we have a personal opportunity to be like Jesus and bridge the gap between ourselves and those we seem to dislike.

Perhaps there is someone you dislike but whom you have to see each day. What would happen if you sent that person a small card of greeting? What would happen if you invited that person out for a cup of coffee? What would happen if you bought that person a flower? God would smile. That's what would happen.

Today you can contribute to true peace on earth, and goodwill toward all people.

Lord, I pray that I may love my enemies, that I may turn my other cheek to those who strike me. I pray that I may extend my hand in friendship and conciliation to those who have lifted their swords against me. Protect me, God, in this treaty of the heart.

Giving Cheerfully

God loves a cheerful giver.

2 CORINTHIANS 9:7

Our cat sits on the deck and sleeps. When she hears the rustle of leaves, or the cry of the mockingbird, she quickly lifts her head up, surveys the advisability of pursuing the sound, then she stretches a bit, curls up, and returns to her sleep.

We human beings also sit up and take note at certain times. For example, I stayed up until after midnight, writing and proofreading, the time moved without my say-so. When I looked up at the round clock, it seemed as if it was laughing, having played a good trick on me, those hands spinning around the numbers without my noticing.

I slept poorly that night, woke up early, drove to work, and acted out the day bravely. When I returned home in the late afternoon, David asked me if I would drive him to the music store because a string on his guitar had broken. So I drove him.

When we returned, Roe asked if I would set the table and pick up Karen at her friend's house. I pulled out the glasses and plates and forks and knives and arranged them on the table, then I drove across town. When Karen stepped into the car, she asked if I would take her to the library because she needed a few books for her report on Kentucky.

The librarian reminded me that I had three books overdue.

By the time Karen and I returned to the house, dinner was ready. Michael asked me if I would help him carry his chair from the living room to the kitchen.

"I used the chair as my helicopter, Dad."

I wanted to ask him if he could have flown the chair back into the kitchen, but I was too tired.

After dinner, Roe and I washed and dried the dishes, then she asked me if I would like to go for a walk.

We walked, or, I should say, Roe walked and I *marched*, step-by-step in a steady rhythm; otherwise I would have fallen over and slept on the next soft lawn.

In the past thirty-six hours I had slept only six hours, and I was exhausted. When we returned from our walk, I had to break up an argument between the boys, give Karen a shower, feed the cat, open the door for the cat, wash out the fishbowl, return a call to the insurance agent, read to Karen, and, finally, read to Michael. David, being the oldest, doesn't want me to read to him in the evenings any longer.

I read to Karen, tucked her in, brought her a glass of water, said prayers, chased the ghosts from her closet, pulled down the blinds, kissed her good-night.

I read to Michael, tucked him in, brought him a glass of water, said prayers, chased the pirates out of his closet, pulled down the blinds, kissed him good-night. I was five seconds away from ending the day and throwing myself onto my bed for the night when Michael said in a quiet voice, "Daddy? Could you get my blanket?" I wonder if, after Michelangelo was washing his paintbrushes after having just completed the ceiling mural in the Sistine Chapel, the Pope leaned over his shoulder and said, "Michael, I was wondering if you add just one more image—something like God and man nearly touching. Something like that."

My Michael wanted his blanket, which was not on the first floor but in the basement, in the back, inside the closet, under the basket. "Karen hid it on me," Michael explained.

I wobbled down the first flight of stairs. I rubbed my eyes. I wobbled down the second flight of stairs and nearly tripped over the cat.

I staggered into the basement, forced my arm to reach into the closet, pulled the blanket out from under the basket. Sleep. Sleep. All I wanted was sleep.

I climbed both flights of stairs as if my legs were made of cement. I stepped into Michael's room, placed the blanket beside him, and kissed him good-night. Just as I was about to tumble out of his room, he whispered, "Daddy, thank you for going all the way down in the basement for my blanket. I love you."

"You're welcome. I love you, too, my boy," I said and then walked into my bedroom, flopped on my bed, stretched a bit, curled up, and went to sleep. I wouldn't be surprised if Roe told me the next morning that she heard me purring all night.

How do you give? Freely or from coercion? And what is your motivation? You will be offered many opportunities today to be a giving person, to have a generous heart. Think before you act: Am I giving cheerfully or begrudgingly? And do I remember who is watching?

God, creator of all things, You have given me life, earth, love. You have given me such gifts in Your generosity. Today I pray that I may take up Your example and give of myself willingly. Help me, Lord, to see who will benefit from my gifts. I pray that I may offer my assistance with joy.

The Garden of God's Delight

Let the fields be jubilant and everything in them! Then the trees of the forest will sing, they will sing for joy before the LORD.

1 CHRONICLES 16:32–33

Roe and I often walk after supper: down the street to the left, through a small path, along the empty roads winding between maple trees and wild grass. At first these walks were for health reasons. We thought the exercise worthwhile.

During the first week we concentrated on our speed and arm movements. We bought proper walking shoes, wore shorts and loose shirts. In the evenings we dressed in white or yellow.

By the end of the second week, we discovered something beyond the measuring of our pulse: each other. One evening we counted the number of rabbits we came across: eight. Another night Roe and I planned Karen's birthday party. One late afternoon we spoke about our favorite ice cream: chocolate. We compared different brands, textures, prices. I prefer soft ice cream; Roe likes hard ice cream, in a cone—a sugar cone.

By the third week we gave up trying to swing our arms in a true walker's swing. We were holding hands.

Last week, during one of our walks, Roe suddenly said, "Smell! Take a deep breath! What do you smell?"

"Fresh air?" I asked.

"Try again."

I tried again. "Freshly cut grass?"

"We have to turn back a few steps. It's gone now." She stopped, turned around, and began walking in the opposite direction. I followed.

"Here! Here it is again! What do you smell?"

I stood next to Roe and brought a barrelful of air into my lungs.

"Honeysuckle?" I asked.

"Yes! Can you smell it?"

Roe and I met when she was twenty-two and I was twenty-four. We had both grown up near the edge of woods that were lined with honeysuckle, and the smell of this wildflower brought the same memory to us: the moment of a childhood pleasure in a long-ago adventure through the neighborhood of our separate dreams.

"Let's see if we can find the flowers," Roe suggested. She began to walk upwind, thinking, rightly, that the scent was carried along the slight currents of air moving against us.

Within a few moments we both stood before a small clump of trees, and at the foot of the trees, in shy repose, sat a honeysuckle plant. Roe leaned over and, like a mother plucking a strand of hair from her daughter's face, picked a honeysuckle flower and placed it under my nose.

"Smell," she whispered.

I drew in the breath of a little god hidden deep within the slender petals and smelled the flower.

Perhaps the fountain of youth draws its power from the pressed juices of the honeysuckle plant, for as I recognized the flower's scent, I was back in the yard of my childhood, stopping between a hide-and-seek game with my brothers and sisters, or on my way after a call to supper from my grandmother waving at the top of the back porch steps.

I leaned over the bush, picked a flower, and placed it under Roe's nose, and she, too, closed her eyes.

When we both returned to our senses, we snapped a few long strands of honeysuckle from the plant, then we walked home.

So far, Roe and I have both lost ten pounds.

We need to share little things with those we love, for in this sharing, we discover more about those we love. God provides us with a huge exhibit in His World's Fair.

Take a friend out for lunch today and walk together. Enjoy the different displays God arranged for your admiration: flowers, rabbits, trees, smells. Tell your friend how beautiful these God-created things are. Your friend will be grateful for your vision and for your company.

I pray that I may be jubilant in the presence of all God's gifts, that I may sing in the halls of God's house: His earth, His garden, His holy place for my joy. Let me be jubilant.

The Memory of God's Gift

I tell you the truth, today you will be with me in paradise.

LUKE 24:43

My wife and I bought our little house seventeen years ago. We moved in during the month of October. The leaves in the tall oak trees had already begun to change into their deep red colors. We didn't know that under the cold autumn earth a small surprise waited for us.

I grew up in a house that was surrounded with a rough garden. I call it rough because there was little difference between the yard and the distant woods and open fields. My father planted ferns, which grew wild at the lip of the woods. He planted raspberry bushes that grew and grew and took control of the entire north side of the property. The daffodils that bloomed each spring were planted by the previous owners of the house. And my grandfather planted white roses that clung to the trellis he built the last summer before his death.

There was one particular flower I made a point of looking for each spring: the bleeding hearts. I thought my mother made up the name. I was startled to see the small, pink flowers that grew in the shape of hearts, just like the ones on the playing cards. Just like on the pictures of *Alice in Wonderland*. I liked to pick a single heart-shaped flower and hold it between my fingers. I liked to pick apart the flower and find its small, white skeleton inside, for that is what the inside of the flower looked like.

One afternoon, during our first spring together in our new house, I was walking in our small yard when I saw, from a distance, a cluster of pink flowers drooping from a green stem: bleeding hearts. I had never seen these flowers anywhere else except in my parents' yard, and here I was, in the yard of my new life with my new wife, and there, waiting for me, were the flowers of my childhood.

I picked one flower and slowly pulled it apart and there, as always, was the inner, white skeleton also shaped like a heart.

We all come from the same roots, from the same soil. We all come from the first love created in a distant garden, or distant desire to be less lonely. How familiar those bleeding hearts were to me. They were simple gifts from God. As is written in Psalm 77:11, "I will remember the deeds of the LORD; yes, I will remember your miracles of long ago." The flowers in my garden were just like miracles, a gift from God—plucked, it seemed, from the garden of my childhood.

Look around in your home today and see what gifts God brought to you. Is it a plant? Is it a photograph? Perhaps one of God's gifts is a particular window in your house that brings in much sunlight.

Select a specific gift you recognize as being a true gift from God, then share that gift with a friend today.

In my vision of heaven there is a whole field of bleeding hearts waiting for me.

With my hands I hold little gifts that bring me joy: flowers, a ring, perhaps a favorite book. With my heart I hold big gifts that bring me joy: faith, love, and charity. I pray, Lord, that I may be a little gift in Your hands, and a big gift in Your heart in all that I think, in all that I say, and in all that I do. Amen.

Things Work Out for the Best

It is fine to be zealous, provided the purpose is good.
GALATIANS 4:18

The plan was a trip to the shore for the afternoon. Eighty degrees. Suntan lotion. Picnic lunch. The children ran around the house, anxious to dodge the ocean waves again. I dreaded the impending adventure. I do not like sitting in the sun. It hurts my eyes when I try to read. It burns my skin.

"Roe," I called out as I began walking out the door, "I'm going to see if I can buy a beach umbrella."

The first store had run out. None in stock. The second store had too high prices. Finally at the third store I found the umbrella and the price I liked.

After I bought the umbrella, the one with blue-and-yellow fish, I carried it to my car in the parking lot of the shopping mall. I wanted to make sure the umbrella was the proper size and wasn't damaged in any way, so I slipped it out of the plastic carrying case, struggled with the catch, then, like a happy mushroom in the moist woods, the umbrella popped open.

Perhaps I looked like a crazed Mary Poppins in the middle of the parking lot. A woman with five children in her van slowly drove by. The children looked out the window and stared. I winked and danced a bit for the children, a dancing bear in the parking lot with his umbrella and his audience. The children in the van laughed. The woman pressed the accelerator and zoomed off. I waved to the distant children, and they waved back.

When I returned to the house, everyone was ready to pack the car and be off.

An hour and a half later, Roe, the children, and I were carrying towels, buckets, blankets, and picnic cooler along the hot sand. I carried my blue-and-yellow umbrella.

The only problem about the New Jersey shore in May is the wind. And the only problem about the wind in May is the cold.

I dug a deep hole, jammed the umbrella rod into the ground, and packed the sand around the base. Then I sat in the shade with my newspaper, prepared to enjoy the next few hours, reading.

The wind suddenly lifted the umbrella out from the hole and carried it off several yards down the beach until I was able to catch up with it. The children laughed and laughed. I looked at them, did a little dance, and they laughed some more.

I held the umbrella high over my head and asked my three children to follow close behind as we played follow-the-leader. Over the dunes, around the snack stand, down the ramp, to the waves, into the waves they followed me and my umbrella. Roe was embarrassed. The children groaned when I started to sing. Perhaps the seagulls were impressed, for they certainly squawked a great deal.

That night, after the children were carried to their rooms, after they were asleep, and as Roe and I were in bed, I whispered, "Great umbrella."

Things don't always turn out the way we expect them to, but if we live our lives according to God's wishes, things turn out for the best.

Live according to God's commandments, and then tonight, before you sleep, recall what happened today and take notice how an event worked out in a different way from what you had expected. Notice how the final outcome was really pretty good.

All happiness, Lord, is Your history, Your book of time spread out before me for my living. Thank You for including me in Your pages so that I may see my part in Your story. I sing praise to You, my God, Author of eternal joy.

Love Your Enemies

But I tell you: Love your enemies and pray for those who persecute you.
MATTHEW 5:44

I remember that when I was a child there was a river not far from where I lived. One of my favorite things to do was to walk along this river and look for frogs and turtles. It was a slow, winding river. I believed that if I listened closely enough, I could hear the river singing. I sometimes wore my boots. I liked to step into the water and swish my hands in the coolness and pull out river clams.

One afternoon, it must have been in the summer, for I remember the heat and the drooping willows, as I walked along the river I saw across the water another boy about my own age. He was carrying a yellow toy boat. It seemed as if it was made of wood. I could just make out a red smokestack. The boy didn't notice me until I slipped and fell into the water.

"What do you want?" the boy asked angrily.

His tone of voice startled me, and I was embarrassed that someone had found me out among the frogs and my river clams, so I just stood up and said nothing.

The boy placed his boat on the ground and picked up a stone. The water reached my knees. I shaded my eyes from the sun just in time to see the boy jerk his arm back and fling the stone in my direction.

I quickly spun around and began to wade toward the shore just as I felt a sudden pain in the back of my head. I reached up and placed my hand where the stone struck me. I turned to face the boy. He was leaning over, lifting up his yellow boat. That is when I noticed my moist hand. I brought my hand down and saw my own blood smeared between my fingers. The boy slowly leaned over and placed his toy into the water. For a moment we both watched the little boat float peacefully along the edge of the river, and then I walked home.

Which boy does the river sing for? I always believed it sang for me. I still do, and I no longer fear the chance that the yellow boat will wind its way into my life.

Jesus urges us to believe that, despite the ugliness of the other boy, the river creates music for everyone. Christ does not exclude His gifts and love from anyone. Jesus teaches us to make sure that, in our righteousness, we don't drown out the singing of the river from the ears of the lost children.

We eventually learn that ugliness can be beaten, not with another rock, but with the recognition that evil exists and in the courage to maintain a desire to help bring all people to the good river.

Perhaps today you can make a copy of this little story and place it on the desk of someone who has tried to move against you recently, and then pray that this person will, once again, hear the singing of the river.

Sweet Lord, have patience with us. We build walls that divide. We close doors to keep others out. Teach us how to topple the walls stone by stone. Show us how to open the doors and bless all who enter.

The Meaning of Inner Peace

The LORD turn his face toward you and give you peace.
NUMBERS 6:26

There have been a number of moments in my life when I recognized the existence of inner peace. We seek what brings us satisfaction: the success of our children, the love of our wives, husbands, friends, a project well-done. Isn't there, however, something more beyond these obvious, well-earned victories?

During an oncoming thunderstorm Johnny and I were riding our bicycles home from the summer lake. Johnny was my neighbor and my best friend when I was a boy.

The clouds blackened. The winds picked up. "We better hurry!" Johnny said as he turned his head and called back to me as I tried to keep up with him—Johnny the strong, Johnny the owner of a beautiful bike, Johnny my friend.

I began to press my feet hard against the bicycle pedals. We reached an incline in the road and coasted with great speed, trying to outrun the storm, the dark storm, the boy-storm, the power that was about to fall upon our heads if we lost the race.

"Hurry up, Chris!" Johnny yelled as he turned down Ivers Place.

This was the moment I recognized happiness: riding my bicycle in the wind with my friend, rushing home to what was safe and dry and stable.

Another time I felt an inner peace was the day I was walking to the Gulf station to pick up my car. It needed an oil change.

The day was warm. The sun was bright. I remember looking at the sky through the trees above my head. My wife and children were home. I was on my way. My hands were in my pockets. I felt somehow like a seafarer upon the world, free, ready to hoist my sails and take stock of my provisions. I felt I could have discovered the Pacific Ocean. Then I saw the gas station sign in the distance, and my reverie disappeared. But I remember the feeling.

Robert Frost spoke in many of his poems about the notion of casting out. Most of his poems have a person in them, and many of those poems deal with people walking out to the field, jumping out from a tree, pushing off, sending themselves into another world. Often, many of the people in those poems also return after the journey is done.

It is in the drifting away from what we know and love that we discover hints of peace. Perhaps that sounds foolish. How can there be peace away from those we love? I suspect it isn't the distance from those we love that creates the inner joy . . . it is the realization that we can go home again, that we can take the ride with Johnny once again after the storm, it is the knowledge that we can take that walk to the gas station and turn around and rejoin what we love.

Perhaps the journey of our death begins with this sense of inner peace, a stepping away from life and love toward salvation that includes, someday, a return to those we love?

One of the places where I discover consistent, inner joy is in my writing, particularly in the writing of my poetry. It is there that I step away from my family, from my career, from my life as a person with a lawn mower and three children, and I am a voice of what has been created over twenty years—a sound of myself singing where there is no song, dancing where there is no dance, dividing my dreams into pockets of passion where there is no passion—but the feeling is there.

Writing poetry must be like writing music: the creation of a sound that is language, developed by listening to other music, by living the music, by accepting the diversity of inner turmoil. We must live in the ordinary world under the gold moon. We have to live in the caves as we hunger for the open fields. We are driven toward what it means to be a human being on the loose, on the way, out racing a storm, inviting Johnny to join us on the deck—"Cast sails! Cast sails! We will claim her power against our bare-chested sails and flee all afternoon before we are called in for supper!"

That is the meaning of inner peace. Children know. Sailors know. Poets and musicians know. Turn yourself over to the run, to the escape, to the gentle walk in the afternoon and recognize just beyond the rooftops is your home, your loved ones, your foundation for living . . . and be glad.

God wants us to be glad. It is from Him that all gifts of peace are created. Step away from your routine. Walk across the street and look at your home. Have lunch in a different spot in your building. Look at your home or your place of work from another perspective and see if you do not feel an inner peace. See if you do not feel a yearning to go home and embrace those you love. This is what God wants us to do when we stand at a distance from the gates of heaven: Look toward God's place with hunger and inner peace.

We will all someday be home.

Lord, let there be peace in my heart. Let me create peace in the hearts of others. Lord of peace, Prince of Peace, I look toward You for Your invitation. The lions and lambs rest at Your feet. Let me do as the lions do; let me do as the sheep do: Live in peace in the presence of Your care.

Brotherly Love

Be devoted to one another in brotherly love.

ROMANS 12:10

I have an old, old friend who was recently placed in a nursing home. Her husband, a surgeon, died ten years ago, and she was no longer able to live alone in her house.

On one of my visits to her new home, a comfortable retirement center, she and I were sitting in her room. I was curious why she looked so sad.

"Well," my friend said, "I've been feeding the blue jays and squirrels out my window here, but then I was told by one of the nurses that I am not allowed to do such a thing."

"Did she give you a reason?"

"No. She just said it wasn't allowed."

After my visit, I kissed her good-bye and walked down the hall to the office. I asked to speak to someone in charge.

A tall, thin man in his late fifties stepped out of his office and asked, "Can I help you?"

"Well, my friend in room eighteen loves to feed the birds and squirrels out her window, and she was told that it was against the rules."

"I'll see what I can do," the man said.

On my next visit, as I pulled into the parking lot, I saw in the middle of the front lawn of the retirement center a new birdbath on the grass and a new bird feeder on a short pole, and I saw my friend filling the birdbath with a yellow watering can.

Because of an act of kindness and love, an old, old woman was able, once again, to feed God's birds and squirrels.

Jesus wants us to love one another. He will reward us for that love. Remember how Mary, the sister of Lazarus, said, "Lord, if you had been here, my brother would not have died" (John 11:21). As a result of Mary's love and faith in God, Jesus proclaimed, "Your brother will rise again" (John 11:23). Because of an act of kindness and love, Mary witnessed the glory of God.

Think of a friend who is experiencing discomfort. See if you can't arrange something today so that your friend will be a little bit more comfortable. Your act of kindness and love will be rewarded.

Lord God, I inherited from Your grace the impulse to do good for others. Please place before me a task so that I may clearly see what is Your will today, so that I may continue to live off Your inheritance.

Honor Thy Father

Each of you must respect his mother and father.
LEVITICUS 19:3

The furnace in my parents' home was not working properly. Each time it was called upon for heat, it coughed up a miserable sound, then rumbled. After my mother phoned and explained the problem, I stepped into my car and drove the thirty minutes to the house where I grew up. My father had, once again, forgotten to drain the furnace.

My father is eighty-two.

When I pulled into the driveway, I was overcome with a feeling of dread and depression. The trees in the yard seemed to droop. The house looked old and worn-out. As I entered the foyer, I heard the television blaring in the living room. My father sat in his chair, reading the closed captions on the bottom of the TV screen. His hearing aid sat on the table. My mother explained that their cat, Misha, was dying, and that the vet thought it best that it be put to sleep the next day. The cat was a seventeen-year-old.

I walked down to the basement. It was cold and damp. As I reached for the string that was attached to the single light bulb, I looked around the dim room: workbench, tool board, discarded wood. This was the basement where my father had built a twelve-foot sailboat, a fort for my plastic soldiers, and a weaving loom for my sister.

My father was a lawyer.

The tools in the basement were rusted; the workbench was covered with thick dust. I heard the loud television's muffled squawk seeping through the floor above me.

After I opened a valve at the bottom of the furnace, I watched the brown sludge drain into a dry, empty bucket; then I closed the first valve and opened the second, which filled the proper chamber with new water. The water level, which hadn't been checked in weeks, was precariously low.

My father was a college professor.

I turned out the basement light, walked up the creaking stairs, stepped into the kitchen, and helped myself to several grapes from the bowl of fruit that always seemed full. When I was a child, my father held my hand in the fruit market and asked me to help him select the best grapes.

My father tells the story about the day he was released from the prisoner-of-war camp in Belgium during World War II. "I had a bit of money in my pocket, and the first thing I bought was a small bag of grapes. I'll never forget those grapes, so cold and sweet."

My father was an editor.

I walked into the living room with the grapes in my hand. My father leaned out of his chair and tried to adjust his reading glasses. My mother sat on the couch petting the thin, dying cat.

Just as I sat down beside her, my father turned and said, "Christopher, your mother and I took a walk yesterday afternoon through the park, around by the old swamp, and we saw the biggest turtle. Bring the children this weekend, and we'll see if we can't find that turtle again." Then he turned to the television and adjusted the color quality.

My father was a writer.

After I kissed my mother good-bye, I left the house, slid into my car, and drove off.

Last month my father announced that he has finally given up tennis. "I can't see the ball any longer. The cataract operation didn't help much after all."

That following weekend my father led my wife, our three children, and me on a grand turtle hunt. We walked single file between the dried bulrush plants, jumped over streams, startled six geese, and climbed the park observation deck.

We returned to the house two hours later with pussy willows, apple blossoms, three types of wild violets, and three smiling grandchildren.

As I gave my wife a back rub that night in bed, I whispered, "It's sad their cat died."

We didn't see a turtle that weekend, but for a few hours I forgot that my father is an old man. For a few hours I stepped along the outer edges of the swamp and tried to hear the turtle's laugh as I stood upon the spring afternoon with my father, expecting nothing more than our being together, and that was good.

I believe that we are born to love. We are born to know the voices of our fathers and mothers. We are born to do our duty according to the father's wishes, according to the mother's wishes. We do honor to our parents in the way we live our lives and in the way we acknowledge with gratitude the love and labor they have invested in our survival.

To honor our fathers and our mothers is to honor God.

Visit the grave of your parents today and say a prayer in thanksgiving for the gift of life they have given you. Or call your parents on the telephone and share a happy childhood memory with them. Perhaps you could mail your father a note. Tell him how much you love God. Tell your mother how much you love her.

God the Father, You gave up Your only Son to death so that I may live. Jesus, Lord, in Your agony, dying, and in Your resurrection You have given me life. From the love of my parents I was born. From the love of the Lord we all have been born twice: once in the flesh and once in the spirit. I pray that I may honor life, celebrate life, so that my soul shall live according to You, my Father, and Your wishes. Amen.

Blessed Is the Man in the Snow

Unless you change and become like little children, you will never enter the kingdom of heaven.

MATTHEW 18:3

Often, before I walk upstairs for the night, I look out the back window and flick the switch to the floodlights outside. Over the years I've startled a raccoon climbing up a tree, a skunk digging in the grass for grubs, a number of cats strolling through the darkness.

One particular late evening, after the children were asleep and Roe was sleeping, I again turned the back lights on. It was snowing. I liked watching the snow fall, suddenly illuminated with my false light.

I noticed that this snow had accumulated a few inches. I grabbed my coat, quietly opened the back door, turned out the yard lights, and walked to the middle of the lawn.

The houses in the neighborhood looked like dark boxes. The trees loomed over me in an accusing fashion. "You should be in bed," they seemed to say with their crooked, pointing branches.

I stooped to the ground and gathered a handful of snow and licked it. Forty-two-year-old men don't lick the snow. Then I stooped again and rolled a snowball into my hands, pulled my right arm back, let fly my missile, and missed the tree I aimed for.

How odd to be in the middle of the lawn, to be in the middle of all the activity of the heavy snowfall and not hear a sound. The silence of the snow.

I looked to my left, then to my right. I checked the empty street, then I fell backward. I waved my arms up and down, spread my legs open and closed against the snow, then I quickly stood up. A snow angel.

It snowed and it snowed.

I began to feel the cold, then I had a final idea. Once again I stooped down and gathered snow into a ball, but this time I left it on the ground and began to roll it in front of me. Within a few minutes my snowball was half my size. A few minutes later the snowball was large enough. I then rolled a second ball, not as large as the first. After I finished rolling the third ball, it was the labor of the next few minutes that revealed the sure shape of my snowman.

I reached my hand to the top of my head and plucked my cap and placed it onto the snowman's head, then I began to return to the house.

After I stepped into the house, after I hung up my coat, I walked to the back window, flicked the light on again and there he stood, frozen in midnight, the image of a man with a green cap, motionless in time, pleased to be where he belonged. I waved. The snowman did not wave back.

The next morning I woke up to the sound of my three children hooting and laughing in the backyard. I slouched out of bed, opened the blinds, and saw the children at work building their own snowmen, three children snowmen standing beside the one I had built the night before.

I clearly understand how lucky my snowman is. Blessed man in the snow. Holy the children as they sing in the midst of winter.

Snow, like the truth of God, cannot be fully appreciated unless you become, again, like little children.

We often feel that we have to play the role of an adult: on a business trip, at a meeting, on the telephone, at a party of colleagues. People who pretend that they are all-adult and not children are false in the eyes of God. There is a difference between being childlike and childish.

We ought to act like the Christ child, innocent before the world in all our power and love that we are willing to share with those who come into our lives.

Laugh aloud today. Invite your boss out for an ice cream cone. Take your children to the zoo and roar like the lion when you see the lion. Send balloons to your husband. Step outside and spend some time on the rope swing. Kick up your legs and swing back and forth and back and forth and laugh in the shadow of God who knows you as His child.

Always be a child of God, a child of light.

Lord, I feel as if I am the same person I was when I was fifteen. I look at myself in the mirror and see an adult, but when I listen to my heart I know I am still the child. God, help me continue to see what the child sees.

The Unexpected Beauty of God

The kingdom of God is within you.

It seems to me that there is a holy pact we make with God that we are not aware of. I felt such a connection to a godly union after I heard reports on the radio that the valley where I live could expect heavy thunderstorms.

To prepare for the oncoming storm, I called the children home from the neighborhood ball game. I gathered their bicycles into the garage. The laundry flapped on the clothesline. The cat sat at attention on the stoop, twitching her tail back and forth. Then I waited.

The sky shifted colors throughout the earlier part of the day, from blue, to white, to gray, to blue, then the wind began to twirl its skirts about the yard.

The oak trees shook. The cardinals and blue jays squawked. A garbage can lid rolled down the street.

I walked to the garage and unhooked a lawn chair from the wall bracket, carried the chair over my head, then opened the chair in the middle of the lawn and sat down. A few oak leaves twisted to the ground. It was my intention to become a part of the storm, to experience what the birds experience, a sudden shower upon their heads.

I leaned back in the chair and inhaled. The air is fresh and sweet at the beginning of a storm. I heard people closing their doors and windows. A boy quickly rode past the house. Then I looked up through the oak trees and saw a yellow balloon with a smiling face pass overhead. I do not know why I wanted to follow the balloon, but I did.

I ran to the garage, hopped on my son's bicycle, and rushed down the driveway. Within a few minutes I spotted the balloon heading north. By the time the balloon disappeared, I was in a wide field at the foot of the small hills that kneel before our little town. It was here in this field that I was able to see the entire horizon. All of Michelangelo's unfinished mural swept above me: gray colors, reds, swirls of white and blue. It could have been all of heaven.

There was no storm. The clouds built up upon themselves. The wind blew against my face. I felt alone as I held on to the handlebars of a child's bicycle.

I wonder if God asks us to open our eyes and recognize the hints of His existence. Who is to say that God doesn't tease us with yellow balloons with smiling faces to lead us toward the unexpected universe of beauty and of ourselves?

Will you dare to take notice of a "yellow balloon" that will pass you today? Perhaps it will be the howl of the wind singing between the molding of the window? Take notice of the smooth feel of a flower's petal, listen to the sound of a child in the neighborhood, calling out to a friend, "Hey! Let's play tag!"

Take a moment to reflect on the beauty of God's universe. Play along with God. He wants you to enjoy His backyard. Tag! You're "it"! And God is pleased.

Look deep within me, Lord. See my faith? See my hunger for Your love? I am a part of the ordinary world, and I am a part of You. Oh, God, oh, simple beauty, I look forward to the day when I am in union with You in the kingdom of Your eternal garden.

The Protection of God

. . . For you will go on before the Lord to prepare the way for him . . . because of the tender mercy of our God, by which the rising sun will come to us from heaven to shine on those living in darkness and in the shadow of death.

LUKE 1:78–79

"The German troops were advancing into Belgium. We could hear explosions. I was so frightened. 'My arms,' I said to your grandmother. 'My arms! I am afraid that they will shoot off my arms!'"

My mother was a teenager in the spring of 1940, and because she was so frightened she, my grandmother, and my uncle fled their Brussels home, crossed over the French border, and became refugees. They didn't know where they were going except far away from the bombs.

After much travel, after much exhaustion, my uncle Henry, my grandmother, and my mother arrived in a small town on the coast of France: Dunkirk.

"There were so many people: families like us, carrying suitcases, children crying, planes flying overhead. And the soldiers. There were thousands of soldiers. We simply thought this was normal, probably what the rest of the world was experiencing at the moment. Of course, we didn't know at the time that the British troops were being pushed to the sea and were stranded, waiting for any possible help their country might, and did, send across the channel to rescue them.

"But we were not troops. We were three hungry, tired people in search of a hotel."

Of course, my family couldn't find a hotel, and it became obvious to my grandmother that they had to leave this city of turmoil. They walked to the bus station, where there were hundreds and hundreds of people waiting for one of the last buses to leave Dunkirk.

Have you ever been in a crowd when suddenly the people from the rear begin to move forward like a wave and all who are in front are shoved?

"When the crowd saw the bus," my mother explained, "the crowd began to push. The bus approached closer and closer, and the crowd increased its fury."

My grandmother saw my mother being thrown under the bus, and she screamed and screamed at the bus driver to stop.

Above the roar of the crowd, the driver managed to hear my grandmother's pleading, and he stopped the bus.

He stepped out and asked my grandmother what the trouble was.

"My daughter! She's been thrown under the bus!" The driver and my grandmother stooped under the crowd and there was my mother flat on her back with the rear wheels of the bus rolled up on the side of her outstretched dress.

"Then the driver turned to my mother and said, 'Because your daughter had such a fright, your family may have the first seat on the bus.'"

My mother and grandmother and my uncle climbed in. The crowd pressed forward, filling the remaining seats quickly, and the bus drove off leaving most of the other people behind.

So much would have been lost in the history of my family had the wheels rolled six inches more: my brother and sisters, my own life . . . my children David, Karen, and Michael.

We are held together with a thin, historical thread of life.

I am sure that God must have wept during World War II. The world seems to cry out at times, "My God, my God, why have You forsaken me?" Chaos, hate, national turmoil is the culmination of lost faith among a whole people. We feel abandoned to evil.

Do not be afraid. In times of your own chaos or inner turmoil do not be afraid to stand up against evil and regain control of your life. Tip your flag of triumph toward God as He stands there waiting for you with His treaties of peace and forgiveness.

God of mercy, when I sit in darkness, remind me to call out Your name. When I am in battle with pain, remind me to place Your hand on my forehead. When I am in doubt, parade the victory of Your resurrection in my heart and mind, for then I will be reminded.

Choose the Weak the Way God Does

God chose the weak things of the world to shame the strong.
1 CORINTHIANS 1:27

At a recent Little League game I was sitting in the bleachers, watching my daughter, Karen, playing the catcher's position.

Halfway through the game, a man with one leg hobbled up to the right field fence, leaned his crutches against a trash basket, and held on to the fence for support.

There was much cheering from the crowd as the game continued. Occasionally I looked in the direction of the one-legged man. He wiped his brow. He stooped forward a bit. I noticed he closed his eyes often.

As my daughter returned to the bench between innings, she looked over and waved. I waved back.

Toward the end of the game, I turned to my left and noticed two little girls walking together. They were, perhaps, eight years old. One girl suddenly noticed the one-legged man. She raised her eyebrows, cupped her mouth with her hands, then nudged her friend, and pointed. They both laughed.

The closer the girls made their way toward the man, the more amazed they were. At one point one of the girls stooped down to establish, for certain, that the man was, indeed, missing his right leg. When the girl stood up again, she poked her friend, then she lifted her right leg and began hopping. "See, I can do it, too," she said, laughing again.

The other girl looked at the man, then she, too, lifted her leg and hopped along next to her friend. They both continued to laugh. After a moment, they knocked each other off balance, landed on their two good legs, and then they ran together to the snack stand.

"Daddy!" My daughter called out at the end of the game. "We won!" She ran up to me from the field, held my hand as we started walking to the car.

"It was so much fun. Did you see me hit? I also tagged the girl out at home plate. The coach wants to take us all out for ice cream." As Karen spoke about the victory, about her favorite ice cream flavor, and about the winning run, I looked to my right and saw the one-legged man hobbling slowly across the field.

"Daddy? Aren't you listening?" Karen asked.

"Yes, Karen. A fine victory," I said as I thought about the man who comes to watch the children play and listen to their laughter.

We can take great delight in a daughter singing about her baseball victory. It is obvious who the champion is just by looking at the scoreboard. But the old man with one leg is a different type of victor.

In our lives God does not create a clear scoreboard. We have to look closely with Christ's eyes and find the athletes of God's quiet team. "Blessed is he who has regard for the weak. The LORD delivers him in times of trouble" (Psalm 41:1).

Seek out the weak, join them in their struggle, for then you, too, can claim a victory.

Lord God of all strength, help me recognize the true power of the powerless, for then I will understand the triumph hidden in my own pain.

The Man Who Mocks God

Do not be deceived: God cannot be mocked. A man reaps what he sows.

GALATIANS 6:7

The foolish man says:

I am not a religious man. I am not a church man. I am not a man of symbols. I am not a man of formal gestures. I do not recite church prayers. I do not bend my head in a blessing. I do not pay my respects to the dead. I do not wash my hands in holy water. I do not accept penance. I do not sing songs. I do not place flowers at the base of the altar. I do not carry holy cards in my wallet. I do not wear a medal or a scapular. I do not believe in prayer. I do not believe in the communion of saints. I do not believe in the forgiveness of sins. I do not believe in the sound of bells at noon. I do not admire stained-glass windows. I do not wish for my children to be married in the church. I do not wish for salvation. I do not believe in salvation. I do not believe in the Psalms. I do not believe in the Bible. I do not believe in the sacred. I do not believe in grace. I do not obey my father. I believe in envy. I seek my neighbor's goods. I do not believe in one God. I do not believe in the days of atonement. I do not believe in the waters of baptism. I do not recite the names of angels. I do not eat of the Bread of Life. I do not guide my children in love. I do not believe in love. I do not believe in courage. I do not believe in innocence. I do not accept my vocation. I will not give my time to God. I will not give my time to the church.

I am dead, said the fool.

Holy God, holy Mighty One, I bow down before You in this morning's sun and say three times, in gratitude for Your love and for the gift of my faith: Thank You, thank You, have continued mercy. Thank You for the Word of hope. Holy God, holy Mighty One, I am alive!

Lighting the Way for Others

When Jesus spoke again to the people, he said, "I am the light of the world. Whoever follows me will never walk in darkness, but will have the light of life."

JOHN 8:12

Do you hold up a light for those you love so that they may see where they are going? Perhaps they do not know that your arm hurts. Perhaps they do not know that you spend many hours polishing your lantern and wiping the glass so that the best rays of light pierce the darkness.

When I was eight, I invented a game with a bottle of bubbles. First I created many bubbles through my plastic blower, then I looked for a bubble that was wider than the lip of the bottle. I chased the bubble, then I caught it with the bottle. The bubble sat on the top, covering the opening. In my mind, my bottle of bubbles was now a lamp with its flame.

Of course the "flame" was the bubble. The game was to see how far around the yard I could walk until the bubble popped, or until my "light" was extinguished.

Each time the bubble burst, I ran back to the front steps where I began and started all over again, trying to beat my previous distance with my light game.

If there is a single truth I wish to pass along to my three children, it is this: "I cannot solve all your problems, but I can *help* you with each and every one of them."

It seems to me that we human beings are built to help each other. We have the ability and the sense to help those in need.

I think about a small boy lighting the yard with his bubbles. I think about the man lighting the path of his children's lives with advice, hugs, suggestions. Those we love best will tend to brush aside our advice quickly, but nevertheless we do not stop lighting the way.

Today make it a point to offer your gift of advice to someone who is in the dark. Perhaps a co-worker is trying to solve a problem. Perhaps your spouse cannot find his or her way out of a sticky social dilemma. Perhaps your high school student doesn't know how to correct a mistake he or she made in school.

What would Jesus do in the streets of Jerusalem if He came upon a person with a difficult decision to make? He would light the way with His words of eternal wisdom. Jesus would encourage the one who is puzzled. Jesus would sit beside your co-worker, your spouse, your son or daughter, and He would offer advice based on what He knows.

God's knowledge is complete. If you imitate Christ in your gesture of help, the right words of advice will come to your lips.

Please, Lord, do not walk too far ahead of me in my journey. I do not want to lose track of Your light. I choose to live in Your light. Let me hold Your robe so that I may always see.

Finding Truth

Truth will set you free.

JOHN 8:32

I read in the newspapers this morning that scientists believe that the Milky Way is being pulled with a super force away from its common shape. I like to read about things beyond my understanding because these things give me a clear reminder that I am not as clever as I sometimes think I am.

During my work as a school administrator I am often asked to make suggestions on teacher improvement. I am asked by parents what I am doing to improve the reading and writing curriculum.

I can stand before a large crowd of people and make pronouncements, recite statistics, explain a reading-and-writing philosophy that seems to make sense to everyone around me, but often a more powerful truth is discovered in the most unexpected places.

I met a third grade boy in the library of the elementary school. He was quietly reading.

"What are you reading?" I asked.

"Just a book," the boy answered.

"What is the book about?"

"A boy in a peach, and how he makes friends with these insects."

"Why do you like the book?"

"I don't know. Because I'm the boy in the peach."

I believe it is better to open our eyes and hearts when we wish to learn simple truths. All my fancy college statistics will not move an audience as much as the story of the boy who reads because he believes he is the person in the book. That is what my real job in education is all about: connecting children to books.

St. John wrote that the truth shall make you free. Look around today for images of truth: a cross at the simple tip of a church, your wedding ring, a neighbor's warm wave across the street.

We have more to learn from what is placed before us than from what we seek.

God in heaven, God in my house, because You taught me to love, because You taught me to see, because You taught me to listen, I am free in Your truth. I am grateful to be Your student.

God and Fairness

Every good and perfect gift is from above, coming down from the Father of heavenly lights.

JAMES 1:17

Each year, during the first week of July, David, Karen, Michael, and I open the garage door, adjust our eyes to the darkness, straddle our bicycles, grip the handlebars, adjust our brakes, and zoom down the driveway.

We coast to the stop sign, turn left, ride for three minutes, cross the main street, and pedal down the church driveway.

The driveway is long and wide, bordered by wide lawns, maple trees, and ... wild blackberry bushes, which no one seems to care about.

This past July, my children and I raced along the blacktop, past the sign "Our Lady of Good Counsel Church." We were going blackberry hunting.

Life, in a way, is like picking blackberries. There are plenty of thorns waiting for you, but if you are careful and delicate and grateful and hungry and patient, the fruit will be your prize.

Michael was ahead of us. "Come on, you guys! Hurry up!"

"The berries won't walk away," Karen shouted.

"I wish they weren't so loud," David said.

Michael laughed in the distance. Karen tried to catch up to him as he made zooming noises like a rocket or like a nine-year-old boy.

Suddenly all was quiet. Karen and Michael were standing before the bushes. By the time David and I arrived, I had a suspicion.

"There aren't any blackberries," Karen said.

Michael had his hands on his hips. "That's not fair."

David stepped closer to the bushes. "There were a lot of berries, but someone ate them all." He snapped off a piece of the bush to show me the empty stem where, indeed, there once were blackberries.

"Maybe a bear ate them?" Michael asked hopefully.

"Nah," Karen answered. "There aren't any bears around here."

"That's not fair," Michael repeated.

"What's not fair?" I asked.

"We wanted the berries. We come each year. It's our secret. They're our blackberries."

"Well, not really," David said. "This isn't our property."

"Well, it's not a nice thing to do, take them all. It's just not fair," Michael repeated as he climbed on his bicycle and announced, "Race you guys home!"

Three children and a forty-two-year-old man were suddenly in the Tour de France, racing for the finish line. Michael! No David! No Karen! Here we are, folks; I think David—no, Karen is winning and, and—I zoomed ahead of everyone and flew into the garage first.

"The winner by a nose!" I called out as I claimed my victory. The children quickly followed, parked their bikes, and ran to the back door, where Roe was waiting for them with a full pitcher of ice tea in her right hand.

At the ten o'clock Mass the following Sunday, Father Pat spoke about the gifts God has given us, then he said, "And let me tell you about the blackberries."

Well, the children all looked at me.

Father Pat continued. "I was walking to the post office. My car wasn't working, so I thought it would be nice to walk. I don't walk much any more. Just beyond the church I found a beautiful blackberry bush full of plump, ripe blackberries. I remember picking blackberries with my mother when I was a little boy."

Father Pat told the story about his mother, then he ended his sermon by saying, "I never got to the post office that day. I stayed in the blackberry patch and ate them all. It was the most fun I'd have all week, and it brought back such memories. God surprises us with all sorts of gifts".

After church, Michael said, "I guess it's fair after all."

When we feel that life and God have been unfair because of events that have taken place, we could remember the words of Abraham when he affirmed God's fairness: "Will not the Judge of all the earth do right?" (Genesis 18:25).

Take one injustice, however small, that you experience today, and remember these words of Abraham.

Take a moment to thank God that you live under His fair judgment.

Though I do not see the final judgment, though I do not see the trials of all men and women, I do trust in Your verdict, Lord. May I come to Your court and be judged worthy of Your admiration.

God and Loss

A time to be born and a time to die, a time to plant and a time to uproot.

ECCLESIASTES 3:2

Last winter my parents' house suffered under the heavy ice and melting snow. The roof above my father's office began to leak to such a degree that we had to carry his books, desk, and manuscripts up to an empty bedroom.

In early spring the damage was assessed by a local carpenter: The roof, the beams, all would have to be replaced. "And the wisteria vine will have to be cut down."

My father planted the wisteria in 1948, the year my mother and father arrived in America from Europe. During the next forty-five years my parents raised six children, planted raspberries, wrote books, drove back and forth from work, and endured the death of their second child. During the regular habits of their lives, the wisteria silently grew along the side of the house and up to the terrace, year to year, blossom to blossom.

"I can't repair the roof unless the vine is cut down. I've never seen such a vine," the carpenter announced.

My mother and father didn't want to cut the plant. The purple flowers, the smell in spring, the beauty of the long, thick vine. Little can replace such a constant reminder of beauty.

After permission was granted, the carpenter, in less than four minutes, cut the vine and pulled it away from the house. Each minute represented a decade that the vine had quietly grown.

After the work was complete, I drove to my parents' home to admire their new roof. I walked to the side of the house. The work was professional. There was no more leakage. The house had recovered from its winter bruise. I leaned over and lifted a portion of the great twisted, gray, lifeless vine. Then I looked up, and there my mother and father stood on the porch, looking down at my catch.

"Your father said he's going to plant a new wisteria on the other side of the house." I nodded as I tossed the dead plant to the side and stepped inside the house for a piece of my mother's sponge cake.

Loss and the acceptance of loss is a regular occurrence in our lives. We are built for such loss. We are also built to endure such sadness, but we will endure because we believe in the God of Isaiah who says that one day our sun will never set again, that "your moon will wane no more; the LORD will be your everlasting light, and your days of sorrow will end" (Isaiah 60:20).

If you have recently suffered a small or enormous loss, remember how things used to be until you can smell the purple flowers of the wisteria, and then all will be well again. I promise you.

I weep and pray. I weep and pray. In my sorrow I carry my faith in anticipation of the joy and triumph that has been promised to me by my Lord Jesus Christ.

Children of the Light . . .
Or of the Darkness

You are all sons of the light and sons of the day. We do not belong to the night or to the darkness.

1 THESSALONIANS 5:5

This is what I saw: a glass bottle about twenty inches high and as round as a cookie jar. It was on display inside a case. The case was made with dark oak and a clean glass front. Inside the bottle, which sat on the top shelf, was a clear liquid and a baby. The liquid completely filled the bottle, and the baby was upside down with its head squashed against the curved glass.

I was visiting a friend who teaches at a university in New York City. His classroom was in the science wing that term. I did not want to disturb his lecture, so I waited for the clock to end the period and for my friend to meet me in the hallway.

As I wandered around, I discovered the bottle. From a distance it looked like a part of all the other science displays I have seen in colleges and museums: a sturdy showcase, labels, bits of information typed on a card and pinned beside the exhibit.

The closer I looked, the more puzzled I became: A vegetable? A heart perhaps? A monkey? No. A *baby*. A boy. His eyes were closed, and a portion of the umbilical cord was still attached.

I remember reading a long time ago a small headline in the newspaper: "Neanderthal Man Liked Flowers." Anthropologists discovered neatly gathered flowers arranged beside the near fossilized bones of an ancient stonecutter.

When I looked at the baby, I asked myself, *Why isn't he buried? Who was his mother? Who was his father? Who squeezed him into the jar? Was the jar filled with formaldehyde first, or was the baby slipped into the bottle and then the liquid poured around him? Why was he placed upside down? How could such a display advance science?*

There is a wonderful poem by the American poet Wallace Stevens, "Anecdote of the Jar," which begins: "I placed a jar in Tennessee, and round it was, upon a hill." The poem is about how a single object can represent the center of all things. "It took dominion everywhere," Stevens wrote.

Flowers were important to men and women of the Stone Age. When I think about the jar I saw placed in Manhattan, I ask myself, *What is important to men and women of this modern age? How far have we come? What takes dominion everywhere today?*

We seem to be seeking the answers to our problems and prayers in science and modernism. The answers to life and its mysteries are not found in test tubes, medical research, and in the courts; they are waiting for you heavenward, in God's hand.

I will not seek human answers to godly questions. I look to God for answers to the unresolved chaos in my heart. ❧

Imitate the Lord

A time to be silent and a time to speak.

ECCLESIASTES 3:7

I asked a friend of mine recently how he decided to become a teacher. He has been a high school English teacher for over twenty-five years.

"My mother was deaf," my friend explained. "Until I was perhaps five years old, I didn't know she was deaf. I was standing beside a lake, and the geese were just gliding in for a landing on the flat, silent water. I began to imitate the sound of a goose, then I turned to my mother to see what she had to say about my goose noise. She was sitting on a blanket, reading a book.

"Honk! Honk! Honk!" I called out in a serious goose-like fashion. I even spread my arms out a bit and twisted my neck. My mother continued reading. I thought she was angry with me, so I honked even louder. I frightened all the geese on the lake and they, together, began flapping their wings, making a noisy exit from the calm lake.

"I watched the birds' shadows move against the water, glide against the shore, pass over me, then the shadows passed over my mother. Only then did she look up. She stood up and waved her book at the passing geese.

"For the first time, I realized that what my mother saw and did were not connected to what she heard.

"When I was a teenager, I asked my mother who was in the photograph framed on the kitchen wall. It is strange how we can be surrounded with things and not know their true meaning. My mother loved antiques. Her kitchen phone was an original piece from the 1920s. She liked farm-print wallpaper. The photograph was of a woman dressed in the clothes of the late 1800s and the early 1900s. I thought the picture just another ornament added to the ambiance of another era created in my mother's kitchen.

"'That photograph,' my mother explained, 'is a picture of Miss Annie Sullivan. She was Helen Keller's teacher.'

"'Who,' I asked naively, 'is Helen Keller?' My mother spun the famous story about a little girl who contracted a fever and was suddenly struck with the loss of her hearing, seeing, speaking.

"'She was a bright child locked inside her sealed body. No one could get in—not her parents, her brother, not her friends. Then a young teacher, Annie Sullivan, came to Helen's house, and from much patience, hard work, and love, Annie was able to reach inside the lost child and bring her back to the world of love. Annie taught Helen language, then Helen learned how to read and write. Helen became a famous woman, giving talks all over the country on the behalf of education, faith, persistence.'"

When my friend entered college, his mother unhooked the picture from the kitchen wall and handed it to him. She wanted him to take something of home with him to hang on his wall in his college room.

"That picture," my friend explained, "hangs between my diploma and my teaching certificate. And whenever I hear geese in the distance, I think about my mother's silence reading . . . reading . . . reading."

God gives us all talents that imitate His work. A mother who loves her children imitates God's love for us, His children. A teacher who inspires his students imitates God's ability to teach us the knowledge of salvation.

Continue today to teach those who need to know, and continue to love those who need to be loved, for then you will continue to imitate Christ, and that will make all the difference.

You are the Resurrection, Lord. You are the Father, all goodness and joy. I look up to You for guidance. I look up to You for instruction. Teach me how to love. Teach me how to pray. Teach me, Lord, how to help others see that You are the way, the truth, and the life.

Our Thoughts Are Not His Thoughts—Neither Are Our Plans

. . . your labor prompted by love.
1 THESSALONIANS 1:3

Do you ever have a weekend that has nothing on the calendar, a free weekend to do exactly as you please? When I arrived home from work on a Friday afternoon not long ago, I was greeted by the children excited about their *new* rooms. Roe had helped the children rearrange their beds and dressers.

"Come, see my room first," Karen said as she tugged my right hand. Michael fell to the floor and screamed, "No! Come, see my room first!"

I was pleased that it was Friday afternoon. I was looking forward to a peaceful weekend. "Michael, hold my hand and lead me upstairs. We'll see Karen's room first, then yours."

As I walked upstairs, Karen insisted that I close my eyes until I stepped into her room. She wanted me to appreciate the entire effect of the new look. "Okay, Daddy. You can open your eyes now."

Her bed now stood where the dresser once stood. Her dresser now stood where the bed once stood. "Karen, I love this. Did Mommy help?"

"Yes," my daughter said as she tumbled backward on her bed and rolled into a ball and giggled.

"Come, see my room!" Michael yelled. "Close your eyes."

Once again I was led into a room. "Okay, now open them," Michael laughed.

Again, the bed and dresser were switched. I sat on Michael's bed. Roe sat on Michael's bed. Michael began bouncing on the bed when I heard a small crack.

"What was that?" Roe asked as she gave the bed an extra bounce.

C-C-C-CRACK! The rear portion of the bed had collapsed.

I stood up and leaned over and looked at the damage. I was expecting to see a broken leg; instead, I saw that the back leg of the bed had broken through the floor.

"I can't believe it! The floor broke!"

Well, that was all Karen had to hear. She began to cry. "I don't want to fall through the floor!"

The mind of a child works in reds and yellows, in light and darkness. A child's fear is a combination of fireworks and mysteries.

"Don't worry, Karen. Just a small part of the floor broke. It was an accident. I can fix it."

The original builder in 1929 didn't join an oak slat against the floor beam. Instead, the wood was held by the grooves on each side of an adjoining piece of wood. When Roe changed the position of Michael's bed, she just happened to place the rear right leg on the weak section of the floor.

I looked at that hole. Michael wanted to see the whole bed crash through the dining-room ceiling. Roe carried Karen downstairs.

Do you remember the scene in the movie *It's a Wonderful Life* when Jimmy Stewart runs up the stairs and grabs the broken part of the banister?

"Yup, yup, yup," I said aloud to no one in particular in my Jimmy Stewart voice. "It's a good thing we don't have anything planned for the weekend."

I stepped out of the bedroom and headed for the basement to see if I had any wood that might fit my weekend project.

My idea for the weekend was simply to relax. This was not God's idea. How do we react when things do not turn out as we intended? Do we become angry? Do we blame God? Take the opportunity today to greet your first unplanned intrusion as a challenge to turn the surprise into a labor of love for God.

Though I work in the fields of my labor, though I toil and carry heavy loads upon my back, I call the field paradise and identify the weight as Christ. Earth is the best place to love the Lord.

Be Cautious in Your Ambition

Fear of the LORD teaches a man wisdom, and humility comes before honor.

PROVERBS 15:33

My father made me a wooden sword from a long piece of pine. I liked the way the tip of the sword was smooth and sanded to a rounded curve and how it balanced in my hand.

One spring, I and my sword entered the woods behind the house where the skunk cabbage grew and the trees were tall and creaked with each movement of the distant wind.

During my adventures, I kept my sword inside a belt loop of my jeans until I was confronted with the pricker bushes attacking my socks or with the creeping ivy reaching out toward my face.

That afternoon I drew my sword and slashed the bushes and vines. I cut the skunk cabbage at the base of the stem and watched the leaves fall like deflated balloons. A boy alone in the woods likes to believe that he is the central power: damming up a stream with stones, pitching acorns at a distant crow, squashing his hard footprint into the soft mud. I was Hercules defending my life against the jack-in-the-pulpits. I was Daniel Boone trying to lure the bear out from under the honeysuckle. I was Merlin turning the bear into my gray cat, which meowed when I called her.

At one point I stood before a dead tree. Its bark was peeling. Its branches were stiff and dry. "This Roman column needs the push from the god of the forest," I called out. I liked to read the Greek and Roman myths when I was eleven.

I leaned against the trunk and began to push my full weight back and forth against the dead tree. Quickly the tree began to sway. It felt like the motion of a horse under me, this movement gaining more and more energy with each exertion from my body.

There was sudden life where moments before there was dry wood standing like an erect skeleton. Then I heard a small crack. I continued to rock the tree back and forth, accepting my near conquest. From deep within the tree's trunk, I could hear more splitting sounds like popping sticks and cracking fire, and then—with a final push—the tree broke at its base with a loud crack and collapsed to the ground.

I drew my sword and crept up to the still serpent and claimed my victory for England and Rome over all that is evil and threatening to little boys as I placed my foot securely on the round trunk.

Then I saw the hole. It was a woodpecker hole, round and dark. I dropped my sword to the ground and stepped up to the tree trunk. I placed my right eye close to the hole and closed my left eye. I could see dried grass.

I placed my index finger into the hole and wiggled my thumb against the outer portion of the tree and pulled and pulled until the outer wall of the tree broke under the pressure of my fingers to reveal the inside of the hole. The light revealed a round ball of grass and seeds and small twigs.

Using my fingers as tweezers, I carefully plucked apart the ball of grass. Small seeds rolled to the ground. Within the center of the nest, I found a dead gray mouse curled up in a ball of ears and legs and tail and fur. The tree's fall hadn't killed the mouse, for it was cold and stiff. *Perhaps it had frozen in the winter,* I thought.

I held the mouse in my outstretched hand. How insignificant I felt. England was suddenly lost. I picked up a flat stone, dug a shallow grave, placed the mouse into the open earth, covered the hole, and then I placed the flat stone on the grave.

I picked up my sword, returned it to my belt loop, and walked home, making sure I didn't crush the skunk cabbages bending in silence to my left and to my right.

When Jesus Christ was born, He taught us humility. He taught us to put away our foolish ways and follow Him. It is difficult at times to recognize that our ambitions are nothing if they are selfish. Power gained without wisdom and love is evil power.

Take a look at your ambitions today. Ask yourself, Do I seek advancement because I am following God's will, or Herod's?

All kings and queens, all emperors and presidents bow down to the Son of the carpenter; bless yourselves with the words from the Father Almighty, Maker of heaven and earth.

I pray that I may kiss the cheek of Christ so that I, too, may be king in the eyes of those I meet today. Amen.

In All Matters of Love We Have Been Instructed

Listen to your father, who gave you life, and do not despise your mother when she is old.

PROVERBS 23:22

Many years ago when I was a child and believed in magic and in secrets in the forest and giants and talking goats, my father asked me if I wanted to find exploding seeds.

I always liked firecrackers, popping wood in the fireplace, a truck backfiring. Somehow seeds and an explosion didn't fit, but I was willing to go along with my father because he grabbed his walking stick, which meant a tour in the garden—which always meant an adventure.

"Do the seeds make a loud noise when they explode?" I asked.

"Well, Chris," my father said as he leaned down beside me as he tied my right shoe, "it depends on what type of explosion you're expecting."

After he tied my shoe, he handed me his walking stick, then the two of us walked out the back door, across the porch floor, and down the wood steps.

Perhaps at a certain age all boys recognize that their fathers are vulnerable, weak, capable of making mistakes, but I continue to believe my father is the strongest man in the world, the smartest, and the best guide during any travel along the highway or through the backyard.

"Christopher, look at the butterfly. It learned to fly just before the great flood."

"How did it do that?" I asked, not knowing about a great flood.

"Well, butterflies have long antennae, and they can sense that water is close by twitching the antennae together."

I also believed everything my father said.

"Well, days before the great flood, the butterfly felt a certain itch between its antennae. It wasn't a butterfly yet, though. It was just a long worm with wide flapping arms, much like you look when you wear one of my shirts. The butterfly was walking along like this." Then my father pulled open his jacket and stretched it out against his arms like a drooping butterfly, then he crouched down a bit and made a slow butterfly walking sound, something like *Smoosh! Swish! Smoosh! Swish!*

"As the butterfly walked along the road that day, it felt this itch between its antennae and said to itself, 'It's going to rain soon for a long time.' And the butterfly knew it was in trouble."

You can imagine what such a story meant to a little boy walking along the side of his father. I had forgotten that he was taking me to see some exploding seeds.

"When the first raindrop hit the butterfly, it jumped in fright. When it was hit again with another raindrop, the butterfly flapped its arms a bit and rose off the ground for a second. Each time the butterfly was struck with water, it flapped its arms harder and rose into the air higher and higher. By the time the rain was beginning to fill the entire valley, the butterfly learned how to keep itself up in the air for as long as it liked.

"The flood came, and the butterfly was spared. Ever since that time, all butterflies learned how to fly."

By the time my father finished telling me the story, the butterfly in the garden had disappeared behind the ferns and we were at the edge of the woods.

"Now, Chris," my father said, "can you find the exploding seeds?"

I looked around for anything that had a fuse, or looked like a black bomb like I had seen on the television cartoons. All I saw were little orange flowers in the shape of little cones and green pods hanging down beside the flowers.

"Reach over and gently pick one of those little sacks dangling next to the orange flowers," my father suggested.

I reached over, opened my thumb and index finger, and slowly closed my fingers around the waist of the little green pod. The moment I touched the seed, it snapped and quickly uncoiled. There was no explosion, but I did jump back, expecting something to hurt me. My father laughed. "This is jewel weed," he said. "Say hello to the jewel weed." My father taught me how to speak to flowers, cats, and trees.

"Hello, jewel weed," I said, reaching over and carefully picking another seed. This time it didn't break apart. I gently placed it on the flat of my hand, then I touched it with my finger until it sprang open.

"Exploding seeds, Christopher," my father said as he began walking back to the house. I watched him walk ahead of me as the butterfly reappeared and flew around his head. I was sure the butterfly said hello to my father, for he answered back, "Hello. Yes, it is a beautiful day."

The butterfly floated across the yard and rested on a yellow flower, and my father waved his walking stick in the air, calling me in for supper.

We sometimes forget where we learn our lessons. We sometimes are not sure how we became the person we are today. Just as God "caused his wonders to be remembered" (Psalm 111:4), so, too, those we love have caused us to remember those simple wonders that today keep us at peace with the Lord.

Praise the Lord who helps us see the jewels in the sand, and who helps us hear the music in the silence. Give thanks to the Lord who helps us taste the bread when we are hungry, and who helps us feel His hand when we are alone. Praise God. Amen.

Good Friday

Anyone who does not take his cross and follow me is not worthy of me.
MATTHEW 10:38

For me, Good Friday means silence. When I was a child, my mother and father insisted that, on this day, we children walk around the house quietly. No TV. No radio. No record player. We were asked not to play any games.

I remember sitting most of one particular Good Friday afternoon in my father's small office. He was a writer and spent many days in, what we called, the sunporch.

On that Good Friday I felt alone. I couldn't hear my sisters and brothers. The television was silent. My sister's record player wasn't echoing in the hallway.

I remember sitting on a large gray chair that unfolded into a bed. It was an uncomfortable chair: lumpy and full of springs. I began counting the pulled threads that were scattered on the back portion of the chair.

The next thing I knew, it was completely dark. I had fallen asleep and woke up hours later with a blanket around me.

Obviously it was the middle of the night. The lights in the house were out. No one was downstairs. I was frightened, afraid to move from the chair or to call out for my father into the silence.

Each Good Friday I think about a little boy alone under his blanket with his cheeks pressed against the rough surface of an old chair. I think about the darkness, and the silence, and the blanket my father had covered me with to protect me from the cold.

Christ endured the greatest silence and darkness on the Good Friday of long ago so that we, too, know where and how to carry our own cross. We are God's children who need the blanket of His dying on the cross for our salvation.

How do you carry your cross? Do you bathe your severely disabled child each morning, and watch the cool water run down his arms? Do you straighten out the crooked photograph on the wall of your mother who died many years ago? Do you feel the cool metal spoon on your tongue as you take your medication with confidence and joy that the new day is on display for you?

If you look closely at the routine of your suffering today, you will find your own powerful way of handling this burden.

Lord, I found the straps that will help me adjust the daily burden of my pain. Lord, I found the strength. I found, Lord, in my trial, the way to wisdom and salvation. You have left a clear path to follow. I found the mark in the ground where You dragged Your cross. Amen.

Christ Looks Down Upon You

> *Take courage! It is I. Don't be afraid.*
> MATTHEW 14:27

Do you fear the image of the Lord? I hope not. For as long as I can remember, the face of Christ looked down upon me.

One evening my father returned home from work with a heavy object wrapped under a brown blanket. It was a twelfth-century Russian portrait of Christ.

During his lunch break that afternoon, my father was walking through different antique shops in New York City when he found this artifact made of inlaid blue enamel. Christ's image was cast in bronze.

On the weekend my father mounted the bronze and enamel portrait on a piece of oak he had in the basement, and then he hung it above the fireplace.

The image of Christ looked down upon all the Christmas presents I received, listened to all the conversations I had with my family, and gazed down upon all the hours I spent in the home of my childhood.

When my wife and I married, and we moved into our two-bedroom home, I quietly drove on my own to a local art and frame shop. I ordered a reproduction of a twelfth-century portrait of Christ similar to the one my father bought. I brought the picture home a few weeks later, glued the poster onto a piece of oak, and covered the image with a thin layer of varnish; then I hung my picture in the house of my children yet to be born.

The image of Christ in my father's house is smiling. The image of Christ in my house is also smiling.

Today, as you enter your busy schedule, remember not to fear the Lord. He wants to be with you. He wants to look down on all that you do. He wants to hear your laughter.

"I give thanks to the LORD, for he is good "(Psalm 107:1). I give thanks to the Lord, for He is happy. I give thanks to the Lord, for He knows how to laugh. ～❧

God of the Meek

Blessed are the meek, for they will inherit the earth.
MATTHEW 5:5

Alfred Lord Tennyson's poem "The Flower" contains the following lines:

> *I hold you here, root and all, in my hand*
> *but if I could understand*
> *what you are, root and all,*
> *I should know what God and man is.*

Few people can understand those lines better than the parents of a retarded child.

In my house where I grew up, my mother and father spent thirty-two years holding the crippled, blind, mute, and brain-damaged body of my brother Oliver. He was "root and all" in their hands. They spent thirty-two years trying to understand him.

Do you know how many times a parent carries his mentally handicapped child from one place to another? Or leads him to the table? Or holds him during a convulsion?

My parents were forever lifting Oliver into the bathtub, carrying him outdoors to rest on a blanket in the sunlight, turning him back and forth in his bed.

Now suppose someone could incorporate the gesture of a mother holding her severely brain-damaged child as she soothes him in the middle of the night?

An entire national and international movement has been founded upon the simple gesture of the embrace. "I hold you here, root and all."

No organization I know of illustrates the power of the embrace better than the Special Olympics.

At a recent Special Olympic meet I attended, I heard a whistle. I turned my head to see five or six runners standing still, looking at the starter's gun.

Silence. Silence. *Bang!* The race was on.

Each child began to run. One Special Olympian immediately turned to the crowd and smiled; another threw his arms in all different directions like loose bits of rope. Then, with purpose, he ran into the far distance.

One girl ran with her feet pointed outward. Each athlete ran, walked, or slowly stepped with courage across the finish line where they were individually embraced by official "huggers": policemen, fathers, mothers, insurance brokers, lawyers, foremen, teenagers—all volunteers. I watched the audience lean forward, willing each runner on with an invisible push.

At another event, a girl placed one foot and then the other onto the balance beam. This Special Olympian looked at her coach, asking with her eyes for assistance. Then she looked at the audience, waved, and walked along the narrow wood, step-by-step, in her white socks.

Her legs shook. She turned slowly, crouching, slipped, regained her balance, stood up, turned toward the crowd, jumped off the beam and into the applause of every person in the stands.

What is behind the Special Olympics success? People publicly embracing the very root and stem of life, perhaps.

John, a Special Olympian from Glendale, Rhode Island, said, "I like Special Olympics because it makes me feel good inside to be with other Special Olympians, to know everyone tried his best, and to know that everyone wins and loves one another."

I am startled at the God and man that is revealed to us again and again in the embrace of the Special Olympics.

Lord, I want to be of service to others. I want to help where there is a need for help. Bring to me today someone who is in need of an embrace. Teach me how to become an official hugger. Amen.

Simple Wonders

Stop and consider God's wonders.

Job 37:14

I do not know anything about the habits of ladybugs. They seem to have the shell of a pea, their wings are red, and upon each wing a black dot sits in equal proportion to each other.

I used to believe ladybugs lived in dandelions.

I truly felt sorry for the ladybug who had to hurry home because her house was on fire, and for my birthday once someone gave me a ladybug brush to polish shoes.

My old friend Rosie on Mallison Street once explained that it is the ladybug, not storks, that deliver babies. I read once that the ladybug could help a young girl find her lover. The girl places the insect on the tip of her fingers and instructs it to go home. When the ladybug flies off, the girl is to follow it to the place where the young man waits.

Find a ladybug on your dress and your mother will buy you a new one soon. According to folklore the ladybug announced the best time to begin the harvest and where the cattle have wandered.

A month ago, I discovered a ladybug sitting at the top of the south wall of the bathroom. It hasn't moved once. Each morning after my shower, I look up to check and see if it is still there on the peach flowers of the wallpaper.

Is it still alive? Can a dead ladybug cling to the side of a wall for a month? I do not wish to disturb it. Do they hibernate? What does a ladybug eat? Aphids? There are no aphids in the bathroom.

I do not think about the ladybug throughout the day, but after my morning shower, I look up and there it is again. Does it look at me? Can it see? Of all the ladybugs that ever existed, why has this one found its way into the bathroom?

Superstition says that if you find a ladybug in the house in the winter, you will receive money soon.

Oracle of love, friend of the farmer, charmer of children in the yard. I like what we human beings have done with so many of the things that surround us. We give things names, create myths and stories about them, admire their colors. We are all scientists of a sort, observing what surrounds us.

There is a skylight in the bathroom, and last night I noticed that the moon shines directly against the wall where the ladybug rests. When I strain my eyes in the darkness, I see a vague spot on the wall.

No one else in the house has discovered my ladybug yet. She is my secret.

She is mine in the moonlight.

God created the universe! He created the stars! The heavens! He created the Grand Canyon! Niagara Falls! The Alps! All that is spectacular, God has created. But we can easily forget that God also created the single blade of grass and the smallest piece of dust that floats in the sunlight of your room.

We should not forget that God is the Creator of all things great and small, even the ladybug.

Take a moment out of this day and see if you cannot recognize God's handiwork in the smallest thing: a single strand of your hair, or a drop of water on the window. If you look closely enough, you will discover His thumbprint.

I do not see the world in the cup of a thimble. I do not see the world in the cup of the sea. Oh, Lord, I see the world in the cup of Your hands, for they are vast and deep for all men and women to gather what has been created.

Godly People

Be rich in good deeds.

1 TIMOTHY 6:18

If you want to be a good person, follow these simple rules:

(1) Always give your baby-sitter a dollar more than she is expecting.

(2) If your grandmother asks you to play cards with her, say yes.

(3) Leave the last amount of orange juice in the refrigerator for your husband or wife.

(4) When someone drives past you at night with his high beams blinding you, don't flash him in the eyes with your bright lights.

(5) If your three-year-old child wants to crawl in bed with you at 2:00 in the morning, pull open your blanket and whisper, "Hop in."

(6) Don't annoy your wife by refusing to touch the moon rock at the aviation museum in Washington, D.C.

(7) After you finish driving your wife's car, be sure you readjust the seat so she can reach the foot pedals and the steering wheel.

(8) Change the water in the fishbowl now.

(9) Wash your hands after reading the newspaper.

(10) If there is a wasp flying around your room, don't reach for the fly swatter; rather, reach over and open the window.

(11) If someone asks you for advice on investing money, don't give it.

(12) Turn the shower nozzle to the closed position when you are finished with your shower.

(13) If you live within fifty yards of your neighbor's house, don't hang wind chimes on your back porch.

(14) Do not hang wallpaper with your husband.

(15) Do not hang wallpaper with your wife.

(16) If the garbage can is full, take it out.

(17) If you loan a book to someone, don't expect to get it back.

(18) Let the neighborhood children play on your lawn.

(19) If your five-year-old daughter asks for a piggyback ride down the stairs, give it to her.

(20) Let your wife pay the bills.

(21) Refill the paper tray of the copy machine when you are finished.

(22) When you are at the zoo, don't feed the animals.

The apostle Paul explained to Timothy to instruct the church people who followed him "to do good, to be rich in good deeds and to be generous and willing to share" (1 Timothy 6:18). In this way, said Paul, they will lay up treasures for themselves and for their children.

There are twenty-two examples above. What deeds will you be able to add to the list just before you go to bed tonight?

I do not wish to serve my boss. I do not wish to serve my time schedule. I do not wish to serve money. All that I do, I do for the Lord. All that I serve, I serve in the name of the Lord.

Living a Life of Tenderness

Be imitators of God.

I think I made a profound mistake this past spring. As the freezing air of winter slowly lost its power over the submissive earth, the ants in the northern section of the lawn returned to the surface and continued their building from the previous fall.

The holes in the ground between the fresh spring blades of grass looked as if someone had poked a pencil hundreds of times into the dirt.

Because I didn't want an invasion of ants in the house, I boiled a huge pot of water on the stove. Then I lifted the pot by its two plastic handles and carried the steaming water outside and stood before the ant holes.

As I began to slowly pour the boiling water into the holes, Michael zoomed around the corner and asked, "What are you doing?"

I quickly stopped the flowing water, hoping I could explain myself, but then Michael said, "Hey! That's neat! Can I do that?"

I have tried all my life as a father to teach my children a respect for life in all its forms. At times, though, when no one looked, I stomped on spiders in the basement, sprayed bees in the attic, and boiled ants.

"Let me pour, Daddy." I looked at my son who loves animals, then I walked to the pachysandra and dumped the water.

"Why'd you do that?" Michael asked.

"I think we can live with the ants, after all."

"Okay," Michael shouted from across the lawn as he was already on his way to Mat's house.

The next day, as I looked out the window, I noticed a crow standing in the middle of the ant holes, pecking away at his newfound appetizers. I pushed up the kitchen window and screamed, "Go away!" The crow jumped off the ground with its thin legs and flew off.

At the dinner table that night Roe said, "I can't understand what happened to a patch of the pachysandra. It's all shriveled up."

"Ants," Michael said just before he gulped down a glass of milk.

Jesus had a gentle, compassionate side about Him. He left that example with us, as a pointer toward heaven and toward God. "Be imitators of God, therefore, as dearly loved children, and live a life of love" (Ephesians 5:1–2).

It may not always turn out as we planned it—with the ants and pachysandra and all—but make a conscious choice today to imitate Jesus in a life of love, in big and in small things.

I pray that I may raise a gentle hand to all that I do, to all that I protect, to all that I meet today and always. It is in the gentle hand that I can express tenderness. I choose to survive through tenderness. Amen.

To Dream, To Imagine,
To Dream Again

*Now to him who is able to do immeasurably more than all we ask
or imagine, according to his power that is at work within us, to
him be glory in the church and in Christ Jesus throughout all
generations, for ever and ever! Amen.*

EPHESIANS 3:20–21

There was a box. I do not remember how this box appeared in my
life. We accumulate objects that are created by human hands. No one
can predict the nature of a child's fancy. He will love a crooked stick
from the yard as much as he will be enchanted with a steel and iron
electric engine huffing and puffing along the gray tracks on the living-
room floor.

My box was in the shape of a rectangle about two feet wide and
one foot high. It was the right size for a boy to carry from room to
room, the right size to store metal cars with rubber wheels and fake
rings with glass emeralds extracted from the little machines shaped like
bubbles that sat upon metal posts, waiting for little boys at the door of
the food store.

I kept this wooden box under my bed within reach at anytime, the
best time just before going to sleep. I kept my Superman comic books,
a tobacco pipe I found in the garage, puries (clear, colored marbles—
the rarest in our neighborhood), a trick hand-buzzer, an Indian-head
penny, a candle, my ice-cream stick collection (good for weaving into

small rafts for the lake each summer). All these baubles were kept safe inside my box.

But there was something more, which is usually the case with little boys, always something more beyond what they expected. This box had a feature I didn't pay much attention to at first. Now that I look back, I realize I never understood how much the colorful illustration meant to me.

Open the box, and I will show you my candles and marbles, and more. Now I will show you the picture pasted inside, behind the top— a picture of a tall ship tied to a pier. This ship belonged to a distant time when the wind blew commerce from sea to sea in the pocket of giant sails held together with thick ropes tied to solid masts.

Look closely. Step down. See the colors of the sky? I like the blue and how the reflection of the ship is seen in the water, a crooked image. Perhaps the captain is sitting behind his door. If you look closely, there is a yellow light beyond the small window.

Can you feel the deck? Is it moist under your fingers? Here, gently touch the wood. I pretend that my finger is a man invited for a grand tour. I usually start from the left and walk slowly to the right until the cook steps out from behind this door and hands me an orange. Once I imagined a seagull and turned the robin's cry in the yard into a seagull cry.

It is best to stretch on your back and place the box on your stomach. (It is easier to pretend in this position.) With my head on the pillow I like to gently rock the box back and forth and measure the strength of my ship against the storm rising. I can see—really see—the waves crashing against the hull. There is a small boy hiding in the empty pickle barrel as the wind howls. The captain shouts an order to lower the sails. See? And, as a whale—one can always count on a whale—leaps just beyond the tall ship and harpoons and mermaids and light and rain and thunder, I am afraid, though I don't admit it.

"Chrissy! Dinner!"

I slam the lid shut—bang!—slide the box back under my bed, roll onto the carpet, stand, wobble with my sea legs (my older brother told me about sea legs).

There was a box that held the first lessons on how to imagine beyond my bedroom walls. I haven't sailed upon a better ship, or found a more suitable pickle barrel.

We are the only creatures of God born with an imagination. We can fly, breathe under water, and create music like Mozart in our imagination.

Imagine, today, what it will be like to someday sit beside God and share a pot of tea with Him!

For the power to dream, I thank You, Lord. For the power to create, I praise You. For the gift of the imagination, I thank You, Lord. For the gladness in my heart, I praise You. Amen.

Revelations

Listen, I tell you a mystery: We will not all sleep, but we will all be changed—in a flash, in the twinkling of an eye.

1 CORINTHIANS 15:51

As the jetliner flew south, I sipped my water and placed the glass on the plastic tray knocking against my knees. I was flying from Seattle, Washington, on my way to Los Angeles, another necessary visit for the writing of my first book.

After an essay I wrote about my blind, mute, retarded, crippled brother Oliver appeared in the *Wall Street Journal*, hundreds of people wrote me letters about the powerless people in their lives. It was my intention to meet some of these people, interview them, and write a book. This is what I did. I flew across the country, interviewed a couple in Rhode Island about their daughter who lived for only one day. I interviewed a family in Washington, D.C., asking questions about their son, Anthony, who was born with half his brain dangling out of his skull. I flew to Ohio and Michigan. In Seattle I interviewed a minister, Dan, who spoke about his brother Paul—hopeless, odd, retarded Paul . . . Paul who suddenly became the powerful, beautiful, brother to Dan. An extraordinary story. A simple story.

After I interviewed Dan in Seattle, I was to make one more visit with a family in Los Angeles.

I sat in a window seat. The plane was filled mostly with businesswomen and men flying between sales. A fellow in a blue suit sat beside me. We introduced ourselves. He was with a telephone company. I was a writer.

During the flight, magazines were handed out, snacks and drinks were offered. I was tired. My trip to the West Coast, my only trip to the West Coast, took place in two days. I left Newark International Airport in New Jersey on a Wednesday, arrived in Seattle, conducted an interview, spent the night, flew to Los Angeles, conducted another interview, stayed the night, and flew back to New Jersey the following morning.

As I sat in the jet on the way to Los Angeles, I flipped through a magazine, not paying much attention to anything. I turned, looked out the window, and there *was* something. I rubbed the glass. Surely there was something in the distance, beyond the clouds, in the clouds level with the plane.

I knew we were thousands and thousands of feet in the air, yet this thing, what was it? Surely this huge object was at the same level as the jetliner.

I turned to the telephone salesman. "John, what's that?"

He leaned forward, looked beyond me and through the window, then he leaned back into his chair with a weak smile, "Oh, that's just Mount Shasta."

"What's that? A mountain?"

"Sure. It's been there for a long time."

My neighbor said he traveled this route hundreds of times before. "I guess you get used to what you always see."

Mount Shasta, a mass of rock and snow ... right out the window. As I drank my water and read my magazine, Mount Shasta grew and grew.

I pressed my nose against the window and watched the mountain pass me. I watched for as long as I could see, until the mountain turned into clouds and mist out my window, and then it was gone.

There is a mystery surrounding my brother Oliver's appearance in the lives of my father and mother, the mystery of our lives leaping out under the mist, the mystery of a force from deep within the earth, causing mountains to press up toward the sun, toward a tired man flying south.

The mysteries of God can confound us, or draw us nearer to him. We have the promise that behind those clouds through which we cannot see in this life God has greater things in store for us beyond what we can explain. "No eye has seen, no ear has heard, no mind has conceived what God has prepared for those who love him" (1 Corinthians 2:9).

Today thank God for the mysteries in your life.

Beyond the darkness there is light. Beyond the empty space there are vast mountains. Beyond the silence there are trumpets. Praise be to the light. Praise be to the mountains. Praise be to the trumpets as they announce the coming of the Lord in my life today. Amen.

We Are Created by God

It is good for us to be here.

MATTHEW 17: 4

Our cat is like a lion, a creature of paradise stretched out on the floral print rug, yawning in satisfaction. Mittens was born in a barn and destined to live a barnyard life, fending for herself, eating field mice, receiving an occasional bowl of warm milk from the routinely milked cows that have spent the day eating grass.

I announced one afternoon to my students in the rural high school where I taught that my children wished for a cat, an orange cat. I asked the young men and women, "Has anyone got a kitten they're anxious to place?" You would think I asked if anyone had warts they'd like eradicated. Every student, it seemed, had a cat, a kitten, ten kittens, any kitten, every kitten to give away happily. Some even said the cats would come with a bag of litter.

I drove to three farms in my quest for a possible creature to adopt. I saw black cats the size of the king's panther. I saw thin, gray cats that could fit through a mail slot. There were calico cats, fat cats, silly cats, sleeping cats. No orange cat.

The selection of a cat depends more on irrational requirements than on sound judgment. "Orange, Daddy. The kitten has to be orange," my daughter explained each time I returned home without a cat.

Orange. Orange. Perhaps I could take a few lessons from Lewis Carroll's frightened deck of cards that painted the discolored roses red to satisfy the queen.

I had two little barons and a little baroness to satisfy, to please, at home. Orange kitten. "You wouldn't want a brown one, or a gold one? Gold, that's close to orange," I asked my children before driving to school one morning. I remembered their answer as I drove up to the fourth farm that afternoon. "Orange, Daddy. We'd like an orange cat."

As I stepped out from my car in the driveway, a man, obviously the farmer, walked out of his barn.

"Hello. I'm Chris de Vinck, one of the teachers from the high school. Your son said in class this morning that you have kittens you'd like to find homes for?"

"You want them all?" the father asked.

I looked toward the barn with its yawning door. Cats and kittens tumbled, rolled, ran, stalked out from the door as if they were in a grand parade. Then, as if on cue, out pranced the picture my daughter had torn out of a magazine. An orange kitten.

"What about that one?" I asked the farmer.

"Take them all, if you'd like."

As I drove home, the kitten didn't cry once; rather, it stood on the right seat and watched the trees pass overhead. She looked at me several times wondering, perhaps, what type of strange barn I was.

When I arrived home, the children greeted me in the driveway. I lifted the kitten out of the car and handed it to six reaching hands.

"Look! It's orange!"

"Is it a boy or a girl?"

"Can I sleep with it?"

"It's a girl," I said.

"It has white paws."

"Let's name her 'Mittens'!"

So "Mittens" it was.

Stretched out on the smooth plains of the living-room carpet, an orange cat sleeps on its back with its paws in various positions and its head turned to a comfortable position. The children are sleeping. I can see small red flowers in the carpet's design. Yellow flowers. Green and blue. Mittens opens her eyes, blinks once, and returns to her dream of haystacks and field mice.

In Genesis 1:24–25 it is written that "God said 'Let the land produce living creatures according to their kind: livestock, creatures that move along the ground, and wild animals, each according to its kind.' And it was so. God made the wild animals according to their kinds, the livestock according to their kinds, and all the creatures that move along the ground according to their kinds. And God saw that it was good."

God created the animals in the world for our joy. It is easy to take for granted a single sparrow jumping back and forth in the bushes. Can you imagine a world without any animals at all: no whales, no crickets, no geese, no squirrels, no armadillo, no orange kittens?

"It is good for us to be here," St. Matthew wrote. The very first animal you see today look at as if you are seeing it for the first time. Take great delight in what you see. Take great delight in its Creator.

Dear God, You created me in Your own image. Am I the image of the Lord, the face of Your love? I pray that I take delight today in all You have created, for there is no greater work than the work from Your hands. It is good to be in Your house. Amen.

Missing God's Blessing

Sons are a heritage from the LORD, children a reward from him.
Like arrows in the hands of a warrior are sons born in one's youth.
Blessed is the man whose quiver is full of them.

PSALM 127:3–5

I had finally had it. The children were loud, cranky, impossible. I was tired and fed up. My wife was tired and fed up. I decided that I was going to run away from it all and have a day just for me. I wanted to spoil myself. I wanted to have a day in which I did just what I wanted to do. I was going to live it up and be as greedy as I pleased. I wasn't going to tend to anyone except myself.

I zoomed out of the house with fifty dollars. *There! I did it!* I said to myself as I drove to the highway and headed north.

Well, I drove to a mall and had a wild time in a bookstore and bought the collected poems of Walt Whitman. After that I drove and drove to a McDonald's and ordered *two* hamburgers, my *own* large fries, and my *own* large soda. I ate everything *without* being interrupted, without giving my pickle to *anyone*, without wiping someone's mouth, nose, lap. Then I bought the *biggest* chocolate ice-cream cone I could find.

I was free. I was out on the town, so I drove to a movie theater and watched a movie without buying popcorn, without someone sitting on my lap, without escorting someone to the bathroom. I was a free man. I was living it up. And I was miserable.

By the time I had returned home, everyone was asleep. As I slipped into bed, my wife whispered, "We missed you."

"Me, too," I answered. I never ran away from home again.

If you are in the middle of the pressures of raising a family, remember, it's no fun being alone.

"Children are a reward from the LORD," wrote the psalmist. So take the kids today to McDonald's, or to a bookstore, or to the movies. Take them anywhere except out of your heart.

Lonely in my heart, Lord. Lonely in my heart. I am not lonely in my heart because of the children on the swing, the children under the blankets, because of the children in the house, the house of the Lord, my Lord, You who have blessed me with the children, Lord, the children. I am not lonely. Amen I say to You with gratitude for the children. For this I pray. Amen.

Encouragement
That Goes On and On

May our Lord Jesus Christ himself and God our Father ... encourage
your hearts and strengthen you in every good deed and word.
2 THESSALONIANS 2:17

Many years ago, after I decided to write a column for newspapers on a weekly basis, I sent out a number of letters to different editors, wondering if they would be interested in my work. I sent them copies of articles I had printed in national journals and excerpts from my books. After a few weeks I was invited to submit my columns to ten newspapers across the country.

The very first column appeared in a newspaper in Albany, New York. From that point, my essays appeared regularly. After a few weeks passed, my first reader's response was printed in the newspaper's letter section.

It was a splendid review. A reader said how impressed she was with the writing, with the perceptions, with the depth of understanding that my columns exhibited. The letter was signed C. Kesten.

On the afternoon the review arrived in my mailbox, my wife was shopping. When she returned, I said, "Roe, look at this first response from one of my new readers!" I was excited that *someone* liked what I was writing.

Roe sat at the kitchen table, read the letter in the newspaper, turned up to me, and smiled. I smiled. Then she started to laugh.

"Chris! Your mother wrote that!"

"My mother! How do you know?"

"C. Kesten. Whom do you think that is?"

"My mother's maiden name was *Kestens*, with an *s* at the end. You know that."

"Well," Roe said with another smile, "sounds like your mother to me."

I phoned my mother right away. "I couldn't resist," she said with a wonderful voice of joy and humor.

So my very first review of praise about my writing came from my mother. I've won awards for my writing, given many talks about writing, had books published since, but no review will ever top the one from my mother in that Albany newspaper of many years ago.

Encouragement. It lasts for a day. For a day. For a lifetime. "May our Lord Jesus Christ himself and God our Father, who loved us and by his grace gave us eternal encouragement and good hope, encourage your hearts and strengthen you in every good deed and word" (2 Thessalonians 2:16–17).

As you think about all the encouragement God has given to you in your lifetime so far, perhaps you can think of someone who could use a simple word of encouragement from you today. Is someone about to make a presentation? Is someone going to be taking a test? Is someone you know going on a job interview?

We all take risks at times for the betterment of ourselves and those around us. Like Christ in the Garden of Gethsemane, we also all need human and divine encouragement to be who we were sent to be upon this good earth.

Lord God, in my race against evil, as I weave around selfishness, as I run past anger, as I begin to lose energy around the track of my life, I clearly hear You applauding for me in the audience, which gives me the courage to complete my race in victory. For this I am thankful. Amen.

The Hope of God

And hope does not disappoint us, because God has poured out his love into our hearts by the Holy Spirit, whom he has given us.
ROMANS 5:5

My nine-year-old son Michael requested stars for his birthday. He asked for an entire universe: shooting stars, constellations. "You can throw in Saturn and the moon, too."

I asked Michael how he thought up the idea of hoping for the universe for his birthday.

"I don't want the universe. I just want stars on my ceiling. Remember at that store."

I had forgotten.

"You remember, Daddy. The store where we saw the dinosaur coloring book and the telescopes? Remember? There were these long, hollow sticks from Africa with beans inside. Remember when we turned the stick upside down and it sounded like there was a waterfall in the stick?"

I remembered.

"On a shelf I found stars in a plastic bag. You can stick them on the ceiling. They glow in the dark. Stars. That's what I'd like for my birthday."

Did you ever wish for something extraordinary? A fancy house? A new car? Lots of property? Perfect health? A child? A husband or wife?

Peace of mind? Michael said the other day that he is saving his allowance.

"What for?" I asked.

"A dolphin. When I have enough money, I'm going to build a huge pool and buy a dolphin."

How can we control our imagination? How can we match what we hope for with what we have?

What are your plans for the day? A walk? A busy schedule at work? Tending to the children? Do you look out the window sometimes and just imagine how things could be different, or better, or easier?

After Michael's birthday party, at the end of the day, he and I walked to his room. We opened the plastic bag and stuck over fifty illuminating stars to his ceiling.

"If you hold the lamp close to them, they'll glow better," Michael suggested.

That is what I did. As I held his lamp in my right hand, I looked like the Statue of Liberty. When Michael and I decided that the stars had been exposed to the light long enough, I placed the lamp on the table beside his bed.

"Let's lie on our backs on the bed and pretend we're outside looking at the stars," Michael said.

I clicked off the lamp. "Hey! Look!" Michael nearly laughed with satisfaction. "They really look like stars!"

We admired the glowing lights on the ceiling. I pressed my hand behind my head. Michael did the same. We two were astronomers, discovering new constellations. Who is to say that Michael and I did not capture the universe in his small room that night?—a boy and his father with their hands behind their heads looked up to what they both knew was wonderful.

We do not have to pretend that we have attained joy and comfort. We do not have to spend the day feeling, somehow, that we have not attained our goals.

Instead of a dolphin, Michael bought a goldfish and a goldfish bowl with his allowance. Best-looking dolphin I've ever seen.

Today, as you think about what you hope for the most, look around and take notice: You probably already have what is good and holy and simple—the true stars of the universe and the true dolphins swimming above and around your heart.

It is the same with our hope in God: It never disappoints. We can hope for certain things, and if it is God's will, those things will come to pass, but if we hope for God, His entrance into our lives is an absolute certainty.

Tonight take a close look at the stars that God and his Son stuck to the ceiling of the universe—and be glad.

God of the stars, God of my dreams, I build the house of my life upon Your foundation: faith, hope, and love. Let us pray that all who build subscribe to the same architect—You, my Lord and Savior. Amen.

Isn't Life Good?

For I am convinced that neither death nor life . . . nor anything else in all creation, will be able to separate us from the love of God that is in Christ Jesus our Lord.

ROMANS 8:38–39

When my father was a college professor, a young student from China, a Mr. Tong, enrolled in his class. After a few months, my father learned that Mr. Tong was married, had three small children, and was thousands of miles from home.

My father invited this young man to our house for many weekends. Each time he came, Mr. Tong would become more and more at ease with my family.

We all learned that he planned to earn his degree in economics and then return to China to be reunited with his family. Unfortunately, the government of China endured a great upheaval, and Mr. Tong could not return to his country. For twenty-five years Mr. Tong wrote to his family. Eventually, the Chinese government endured, again, another upheaval, and Mr. Tong was able to bring his wife and children to the United States.

For all those lonely years, Mr. Tong remained faithful to his wife. When he was reunited with her, he later said that they had to become reacquainted all over again for it was almost as if they were strangers.

Today all of Mr. Tong's children are graduates of the best universities in this country. Mr. Tong is a grandfather many times over. He still visits my parents. "Isn't life good?" he will say often.

Remember the famous words: *To have and to hold from this day forward, for better, for worse, for richer, for poorer, in sickness and in health, to love and to cherish, till death us do part.*

Mr. Tong was able to cherish. He was able to hold on to his love for his wife for all the years they were apart. God's love is able to hold on to us His bride, the church, in spite of any difficulties, too. "For I am convinced that neither death nor life, neither angels nor demons, neither the present nor the future, nor any powers, neither height nor depth, nor anything else in all creation, will be able to separate us from the love of God that is in Christ Jesus our Lord" (Romans 8:38–39).

If there is a small break between you and someone you love, think of Mr. Tong, and try to patch things up today. And if it seems that there is a break between you and God, remember, the Bible says that such a break is not possible.

"Isn't life good?"

God of love, thank You for Your hand in mine, thank You for Your love that binds me to Your promise, the promise of heaven, the promise of peace.

Such love is grace, my life is grace, a gift from You, my God. Amen.

He Restores My Soul

He makes me lie down in green pastures, he leads me beside quiet waters, he restores my soul.

PSALM 23:2–3

In the first year of our marriage, Roe and I bought an antique regulator clock. It will run for seven days with a full winding of the spring. During the first week, after we hung the clock on the wall, I couldn't sleep well. I dislike the sound of ticking. It drums into my head. I count each ticktock. My efforts to sleep were useless.

For two years, each time we were ready to walk up the stairs for the night, I stopped the clock's pendulum. In the morning, I'd reset the clock, push the pendulum, and the ticking would continue again throughout the day, until the moments before Roe and I went to bed.

Into the third year of our marriage, I stopped winding the clock altogether, not bothering to stop and restart the thing any longer.

For the past thirteen years the clock has remained silent on the wall in the family room. I like silence when I sleep. We have an electric clock. Water doesn't drip in the bathroom. Silence is a luxury.

My friends and my children often ask why I don't get my clock fixed. I say again and again that it is working just fine.

We have to sometimes arrange our lives according to our own needs. It is good to be generous, giving, loving, but it is also good, every now and then, to treat ourselves.

Jesus set this example, for Himself and for those who followed Him. In the middle of the press and crush of need, He turned His disciples' attention toward their own concerns. "Because so many people were coming and going that they did not even have a chance to eat, he said to them, 'Come with me by yourselves to a quiet place and get some rest'" (Mark 6:31).

Today might be a good day to rearrange something in your life that will bring you a little comfort and peace.

The sun keeps me warm, and the evening mist of summer keeps me cool. When I am hungry, bread and fish keep me from hunger. But no sun, no wind, no food has brought me as much warmth, fresh air, and comfort as Your love for me, Lord God of the sun, God of the air, God of the smallest grain of rice.

In the Image of God

So God created man in his own image, in the image of God he created him; male and female he created them.

GENESIS 1:27

What habits do you cherish? Do you like to sit before the mirror in the evening and unpin your hair? Do you brush your hair a certain number of times? When you look in the mirror, do you think about the changing face that you see? Do you remember when you were young? Do you remember when you stood before the mirror and feared that you might not be attractive? Do you remember looking deep into the image that looked back at you and you wondered if what you saw was real?

My mother had a long mirror in her bedroom. I nearly believed that I could walk through this mirror and join Alice and the White Rabbit and the Mad Hatter.

I remember watching my mother adjust her hair with pins and combs. My mother kept in a dresser her long, blonde curls that were cut when she was a teenager.

I watch Roe dry her hair each morning. I watch as she brushes her wet hair. I watch as she rubs her dark hair with a towel until her day-image appears.

Beauty is the product of the eye and heart. Without an image there is nothing. Without love there is nothing. Self-love begins with a close look in the mirror and an acceptance that what we see is beautiful and good. After such an experience, what remains during the day is beautiful and good.

The belief in God's unconditional approval of who we are and what we look like comes from knowing what God says about us, His extraordinary creative act: "I praise you [God] because I am fearfully and wonderfully made; your works are wonderful, I know that full well" (Psalm 139:14).

At night, before you sleep, brush your hair, feel the texture, remember the hands that caressed it: a mother, a child perhaps, a husband, a wife. Place the brush and comb down gently on the dresser and lie in bed. Rest your head on the pillow and dream about the mirror, the image maker, for it reflects the sculpture—you—that God has created.

Lord God, Creator of things seen and unseen, I am the clay between Your hands, the stone at the tip of Your chisel. I am the artist's masterpiece, for You are the Master and I am Your creation. Let no one criticize Your work. I am wonderfully made.

Paradise

In the middle of the garden w[as] the tree of life.

GENESIS 2:9

In the house where I grew up there was a large oak table in the living room. This was the table that was once in a great chateau in Belgium where my father grew up. When he immigrated to this country with my mother in 1948, among the items he brought over the ocean was this table.

For as long as I can remember, this table stood in the living room. I know it has been in the same spot for over forty-five years.

The only radio in the house sat on this table. I used to listen to cowboy songs on Saturday afternoon from that green radio. I'd sprawl myself on the tabletop, adjust the radio dial, and listen to a distant voice accompanied by a jumping guitar tune.

This table was the table my father used when he wrote many of his books. I remember hundreds of typed papers scattered about on the hard surface. I remember my father leaning over these papers as if he was weeding the garden with great care.

There was something else about the living-room table that pleased me when I was a child. The legs were large, round, and connected to each other with a thick, wide band of solid oak that had fancy grooves in the entire length. These grooves were perfect for rolling marbles. I remember placing the marbles in a row in these grooves and pushing them along as I pretended the marbles were train cars bumping into each other.

Perhaps it is not true that I spent hours at a time under the table, pushing the marbles back and forth along those thin grooves in the wood, but in today's memory it seems like hours. I sometimes wish that I could return to the table and push the marbles while my mother and father read aloud, or my brother plays a song on the piano, or my sister quietly paints on a paper bag in the kitchen.

Paradise is a memory away, just within our grasp. Reach out and it will become what is real.

I would like to return to my childhood and relive what it felt like to hold glass marbles in my hand while stew cooked in the kitchen pot and my mother called us in to wash our hands, and my father pulled off his glasses and placed them on top of his papers that covered the table. I like the times when we were all together—my sisters, my brothers, and I. When I am tired, I like to think of these times. Perhaps that is what God has in store for us: a place where we are all together with the Father as we rush to dinner where the sounds of His house are full of delight.

Think about the first Tree of Life that is written about in the book of Genesis. And think about the last Tree of Life written about in the Bible's last book: "To him who overcomes, I will give the right to eat from the tree of life, which is in the paradise of God"(Revelation 2:7).

In addition to my memories that God will return to me again in paradise, I take delight in knowing He will give me the Tree of Life.

I remember my father's horn-rimmed glasses. I remember the place of my childhood. I believe heaven is full of smells of fresh stew and the voice of my mother calling us in for the evening meal.

I can still hear the glass marbles ticking and clicking against themselves as they rattle along the grooves of the hard wood. I think God has those glass marbles waiting for me.

Today remember some of your happiest memories, for then you will have a glimpse of paradise.

Lord God, I remember my home, for my home was a place of comfort and peace. Now I am on my way to Your house. I have read Your invitation in the Bible. I received Your invitation delivered to my heart. I am coming. Please guide me so that I do not lose my way. Amen.

Lord of the Brokenhearted
and the Bitter

He heals the brokenhearted and binds up their wounds.

PSALM 147:3

Open wounds are the source of constant pain. A pine tree bleeds sap. The sun divides the night from the day that causes a constant division between light and darkness.

I knew a man, an only child, who believed that his father had cheated him out of an inheritance. The father belonged to a local charity organization. Each year the father's group raised money to send an ill child to a place of his or her dream: Disney World, perhaps, or the dugout of the New York Yankees, or perhaps to a grandmother's house on the other side of the world.

When the father died, he donated all he had to this organization. The son tried to recover the money through the courts, but the suit was settled in favor of the charity group.

For a long time the son complained about the world's injustice. He often cursed the name of his father.

Five years after the death of the father, the son contracted a heart ailment and was rushed to the hospital. It was determined that the son needed a triple bypass. The son died. In his will it was discovered that he, too, had donated all he owned to the same charitable organization as his father had.

Even though the son lived with bitterness for five years, he claimed a final victory for himself by his act of generosity. But think of what the son's last five years could have been like if he had let in the Lord who heals the brokenhearted.

Is there a wound in your life that you have been nursing, or a grudge you won't allow to heal? Perhaps you can, today, think about how you can heal your bitterness. Pray to God. Ask Him how your brokenheartedness could end. He will give you an answer.

I can see the failures, Lord, in the deeds of others. I can be quick to identify bitterness. Help me accept failure in those I love and in my own life. Help me turn my own anger into a reconciliation, for there is no greater compromise than the compromise of the heart. You are my ambassador. Help me deliver true words and deeds of reconciliation to those who are bitter. Amen.

Real Riches

Do not wear yourself out to get rich.

PROVERBS 23:4

I am reading Fyodor Dostoyevsky's novel *The Brothers Karamazov*. In Book IV, Father Zossima, the Russian monk, says, "Men have succeeded in accumulating a greater mass of objects, but the joy in the world has grown less."

I was reminded of these words when one of my high school students in my English class called out across the room during the first months of class, "Mr. de Vinck! You bought new shoes!"

I was a bit embarrassed, for I didn't realize that the class had noticed that for the past six weeks my right shoe had a hole in the side where my toe had worn through the imitation leather.

Each September I buy a single pair of new shoes, hoping they will last until the following September. I kept this last pair one year and four months. A record.

Have you bought a pair of shoes recently? Fifty dollars! I spent fifty dollars for the exact same pair of shoes I bought sixteen months ago for forty dollars. I should tell you that I also own a pair of sneakers I bought four years ago. Roe thinks I ought to buy a new pair for the upcoming summer.

"They still work," I argue. "A bit torn and dirty, perhaps, but they still keep my feet warm and safe."

I asked my students, "How many pairs of shoes do you own?"

"Eight," a boy answered.

"Well, I have about fifty, but I only wear about ten of them," a girl said thoughtfully. "People like to have new things. I do, so I buy shoes."

Have you ever seen a person in the United States enter a shoe store with worn, ragged, old shoes on his or her feet? When was the last time you bought a pair of shoes out of a REAL need?

There is a wonderful poem by Carl Sandburg called "Happiness" in his *Complete Poems*.

> *I asked professors who teach the meaning of life*
> *to tell me what is happiness.*
>
> *And I went to famous executives who boss the work*
> *of thousands of men.*
>
> *They all shook their heads and gave me a smile*
> *as though I was trying to fool them.*
>
> *And then one Sunday afternoon I wandered*
> *out along the Desplaines river*
>
> *And I saw a crowd of Hungarians under the trees*
> *with their women and children*
> *and a keg of beer and an accordion.*

Father Zossima said, "Interpreting freedom as the multiplication and rapid satisfaction of desires, men distort their own nature, for many senseless and foolish desires and habits and ridiculous beliefs are thus fostered. They live only for mutual envy, for luxury and ostentation."

Shoes! Shoes! Shoes!

I bet Sandburg's Hungarians danced under those trees—*barefooted!*

I do not believe there is anything wrong with wanting beautiful things. God created such beauty. But we need to remember that we need to "cast but a glance at riches, and they are gone, for they will surely sprout wings and fly off to the sky like an eagle" (Proverbs 23:5).

There are treasures that please us for a moment, and there are treasures that please us, and God, for all eternity. What treasures are you going to pursue today? "Store up for yourselves treasures in heaven, where moth and rust do not destroy, and where thieves do not break in and steal. For where your treasure is, there your heart will also be" (Matthew 6:20–21).

I hold in my hand, Lord, two things: a pound of gold and the Bible. Thank You, Lord, for teaching me which one has more weight and value. Amen.

Pray for God's Peace

Then the land had rest from war.

JOSHUA 11:23

Each time I visit Washington, D.C., either for pleasure with my family or for business in my career in education and writing, I visit the Smithsonian Institute because I want to touch the black-and-white checkered rocket.

When I was a child, my father told me the story of the V-2 rockets, how they would fly over from the enemy's borders and explode in Belgium. "If you could still hear the engine of the rocket, that meant it was still flying and you had nothing to worry about; but if the engine stopped, that meant the rocket was falling to the ground." The V-2 rockets were flying bombs. They destroyed many homes in Belgium and killed many people.

When I visit the Washington museum, I stroke the sides of one of these bombs of destruction and pray for the families who lost those they loved because of such ugliness. Then I thank God for the long-ago safety of my father.

My father is eighty-two years old. He likes to cut and fold paper airplanes for his grandchildren. My children will never know the sounds of bombs falling upon them, and my father is still able to laugh.

God wants us to love each other. What torment it must be for Him to see people killing people. War is the evidence of chaos, evidence of evil, evidence of the Devil's work. Neighborhood strife or international world wars. There is no difference. If we pray, we and God will be the victors. "He will judge between the nations and will settle disputes for many peoples. They will beat their swords into plowshares and their spears into pruning hooks. Nation will not take up swords against nation, nor will they train for war anymore. Come, O house of Jacob, let us walk in the light of the LORD" (Isaiah 2:4–5).

Today is a good day to walk in the light of the Lord. Think of those who have died so that others may live in freedom and in peace.

Lord, I pray for peace in my heart and for peace in my house. I pray, Lord, for peace in my neighborhood and for peace in my state. I pray for peace in my country, for peace in my world. I pray, Lord God, for such peace for today and for all eternity. Amen.

The God Who Gives

Until now you have not asked for anything in my name. Ask and you will receive, and your joy will be complete.

JOHN 16:24

This past October I taught, perhaps, the last class I will ever teach. I have been a teacher for sixteen years, and now I am a school administrator. The new job means a shorter commute and a new challenge. As I looked back to all that I did in the classroom, I became frightened of my new position. How do I start something new all over again? Did I make a mistake in leaving the classroom?

How do you deal with serious decisions you need to make? I share my concerns with my family. I look to people I admire and see what they did with their lives, but then I still have to make the decision on my own.

I have always depended on that deep-inside voice to guide me in my life. That voice didn't fail me when I was hoping to meet my someday wife. That voice didn't fail me when I sought strength as I tried to teach, write, be a husband and father. That voice didn't fail me when I was hoping that my writing would grow.

Someone once said to me that we should ask God for big gifts and graces. We shouldn't be afraid. We aren't greedy people. We know what God likes to hear. We know He likes us to ask for help, and He *always* helps.

I tell my three children that I cannot solve all their problems, but I can always help them with any difficult situation they encounter along the way.

Change is frightening, but I go home to the same wife, the same children, and to the same cat. They are still there, and I pray to the same God. He's still there, too.

Have you asked God for anything lately? Have you asked Him for something extraordinary? He will not help you win the lottery. He will not help you discover the fountain of youth. You and God both know exactly what things you can ask for. What is the biggest thing missing in your heart? Ask God to help you find that missing part. That deep, personal need is greater than gold. God provides. You just have to ask.

I have been afraid, Lord, to ask You for help. I sometimes believe You are too busy to be concerned with my small needs. Hear me, Father. I come to You in obedience, for You have said to ask and I shall receive. I ask, Lord, for Your blessing. I ask for Your help. Provide, provide, Lord God. You provide. Amen.

Heaven's Gate

For by him all things were created: things in heaven and on earth, visible and invisible.

COLOSSIANS 1:16

Some time ago a crow discovered the rabbit's nest that was carefully hidden in the periwinkle. As Roe and the children and I were sitting in the family room, we heard a loud squeal. Looking through the window, we saw the crow flip a two-week-old rabbit out of the nest and onto the grass. The children, my wife, and I gave a loud scream as we rushed outside and chased the crow away.

The rabbit died. Five-year-old Karen wanted to help me bury the creature. She grabbed her blue plastic sandbox shovel. I pulled the spade out from the garage.

After we quickly dug a grave under the rhododendron, I placed the rabbit in a paper towel.

"Can I put him in the hole?" Karen asked.

"Of course you can."

Karen and I stooped down. Just as she was about to place the rabbit into the open ground, she turned up to me and asked, "Can I kiss him first?"

"Of course you can kiss him." And Karen kissed the paper towel that contained the lifeless shape; then she lowered her hand into the hole and placed the rabbit among the roots and moist earth.

"Is he thirsty now?" Karen asked.

"What's that, Karen?"

"When you die, are you thirsty?"

"Sure. And there's plenty to drink in heaven."

We covered the rabbit with the dark soil. I was about to place a large flagstone over the grave, but Karen didn't like that. She couldn't tell me why, but she did want to place a cross made of two twigs over the grave. This is what we did.

As we walked back into the house, Karen's small hand felt warm and strong in mine.

I will leave fancy theories of life and death to the scientists, and I will leave myth-making to ancient people. Karen and I solved the problem in a single afternoon: Rabbits drink in heaven.

Children need to be told of God's promise of salvation. Children need to know from the voice of those they love that Christ will be beside them all their lives, easing their journey toward God's eternal embrace.

In a way you are also a child, a child of Christ. Listen as He tells you of His promise. Feel His presence beside you as you walk through your day.

Think today about who will lead you toward God's embrace: the Lord Jesus Christ, your guide, your Father. Believe in Him and all things shall be reconciled in eternal happiness.

You have eased my way, O Lord. You have eased my way to heaven with Your love and promise. You have eased my way to salvation. Alleluia, alleluia. You have eased my way.

The God of All Comfort

As a mother comforts her child, so will I comfort you.
ISAIAH 66:13

Someone told me the other night about a Tolstoy story called "The Lament." It is a simple story about an old man who drives a horse and buggy for hire through the city.

The story goes that the old man's son died recently and he wants so desperately to tell someone.

A wealthy man hires the horse and buggy for a ride across town. As the wealthy man steps into the carriage, the old man says, "My son, my son. Let me tell you about my son." But the busy man doesn't have time to listen.

Well, after the wealthy man leaves, another man steps into the carriage. He wants to be driven to the other side of the city. Again, the old man says, "My son. My son. Let me tell you about my son." And again, this second man also doesn't bother to listen.

At the end of the day, the old man returns to the stables, unhitches his horse, and as he begins to brush the horse down for the night, the old man begins to tell the horse, "My son. My son." And he tells the horse the tragic story.

Isn't it wonderful that you are never alone, especially when you need comfort during your difficult times? "Praise be to the God and Father of our Lord Jesus Christ, the Father of compassion and the God of all comfort, who comforts us in all our troubles, so that we can comfort those in any trouble with the comfort we ourselves have received from God" (2 Corinthians 1:3–4).

We need to speak about our grief. We need to release our sorrow. This old, simple man in the story knew he had something important to say. We are all poets. We all have extraordinary things to say about very ordinary but very important things in our lives.

Are you keeping something bottled up inside of you this morning? Share your grief with someone. It will make a difference. Or make yourself available to someone today who has recently been given a new burden of sadness. You have the ability to comfort and be comforted.

The substance of my sorrow is the substance of my peace. Help me, Father in heaven, to turn a neighbor's grief to a newfound wisdom: You, God of comfort, God of the embrace. Teach me how to soothe as You have soothed me. Amen.

A Clue to Happiness

How can this be?

JOHN 3:9

When I was a child, my grandmother told me the story about the doorbell.

"Christopher, when I was a little girl in Belgium, there was a wealthy woman who lived down the street.

"This woman," my grandmother continued, "had fancy oil lamps, maids, and a cook. One day there was a rumor in the neighborhood: 'The rich lady, she's got a bell in her door.'"

My grandmother explained to me that this rich woman was the first person on her street to have an electric doorbell installed in her house. I remember my mother's saying that all the children ran to the house, *knocked* on the woman's door, and asked permission to ring her bell.

"Well," my grandmother said, "we rang that bell all afternoon, it seems to me."

I was reminded of my grandmother's story this afternoon as I listened to Nikolay Rimsky-Korsakov's "Procession of the Nobles."

I sat at my desk with my eyes closed and listened to the music when suddenly I heard a distant voice.

"What are you doing, Daddy?" Karen, my seven-year-old daughter, asked as she entered the room.

"I'm listening to wonderful music."

"It sounds like kings dancing," Karen said as she sat on my lap. As the recording ended, she asked, "Can we listen to it again?"

We sat together, my daughter and I, for nearly an hour listening to the same piece of music over and over again. That is a clue to happiness. When you come across something wonderful, like the sound of a doorbell, or a beautiful symphony, stick with it, surround yourself with the beauty you discovered. Share the beauty again and again with those you love.

I carried my daughter in my arms up to her bedroom where, after a prayer and a small kiss, she quietly slept.

"Be happy, young man, and let your heart give you joy in the days of your youth. Follow the ways of your heart and whatever your eyes see" (Ecclesiastes 11:9). You can maintain your youth by seeing things as children see them: with delight. Be happy. It is God's will.

"Rejoice in the Lord always. I will say it again: Rejoice! Let your gentleness be evident to all"(Philippians 4:4–5).

The more you surround yourself with beauty, the more beauty you will see. The more you rejoice in the Lord, the closer He will be to your heart. Today, rejoice!

To You I sing. To You I dance. To You I lift up my arms in honor and delight. Come to me in my singing. Come to me in my dance. Come to me, Lord Jesus. The celebration is at hand. Amen.

Little Children
and the Kingdom of Heaven

I tell you the truth, unless you change and become like little children, you will never enter the kingdom of heaven.

MATTHEW 18:3

Mrs. Robbins had a flat basket attached to her front door, a brown basket in the shape of a pouch; a large pocket, a place for notes, I figured. Mrs. Robbins also had a bell to the right of her door, a bell with a string. Standing before Mrs. Robbins' door was a small adventure for a boy of eight.

Do I pull the bell, or write her a note? I didn't have important things to say when I was eight. I remember posting Mrs. Robbins' acorns in her mail basket and ringing her bell just to say hello. She always answered the door with a loud, pleasing Southern accent. "Hello, Christopher."

It was rumored that Mrs. Robbins' grandfather was once a wealthy landowner in Tennessee.

"What can I do for you today?"

Mrs. Robbins was one of the few adults in my childhood memory who treated me like an adult. I'd hook my thumb in my pants pocket, stand tall, and say, "Hello, Mrs. Robbins." Then I'd stand there not wanting to admit I had mailed her acorns, or that I just liked ringing her front bell.

She'd walk out of the house and sit down on her stoop. I'd sit beside her, and she'd tell me about the possum she found in her garbage can that morning, or about the cookies she was baking in the kitchen. When you are eight, it is difficult to decide which is the better topic: possums or cookies.

I'd dig the heel of my right shoe in the dirt, or scratch a scab on my arm as I, too, explained important things to Mrs. Robbins: the color of my bedroom, or the arrival date of my grandparents from Belgium.

"Would you like to come inside for a while and have cookies and milk with me?" Mrs. Robbins would ask. "Ginger cookies?"

I always knew they'd be ginger cookies, usually in the shape of animals.

"Sure!"

Possums, grandparents, acorns, baskets. Let us not ignore the children who walk into our lives. Let us not forget the taste of ginger cookies.

Mrs. Robbins acted like Jesus. He is full of enthusiasm for simple things, full of delight when a child sits beside Him, full of an inner peace that affects all who meet Him. Jesus wouldn't shoo away a child knocking at His door. "Whoever welcomes a little child like this in my name welcomes me" (Matthew 18:5).

Today take delight in the children. Share their enthusiasm for little things. Call your grandchild on the phone and invite him to a slumber party at your house this weekend. Pick up your daughter after school today and take her out for an ice cream cone. Be like Christ and welcome the children.

Dear Lord, thank You for my memories of my childhood. Thank You for letting me be childlike and not childish. I am who I was as a child. I am who I am today: man-child, woman-child. How good it is to be human. How good it is to be welcomed by You when I stand at Your door and ring the bell.

Little Things, Big Differences

Let no debt remain outstanding, except the continuing debt to love one another, for he who loves his fellowman has fulfilled the law.
ROMANS 13:8

My family and I spent a week in Disney World in Florida last summer. We traveled through Peter Pan's world, dived in a submarine, were chased by pirates, hugged Goofy. We visited Epcot Center and were transported through outer space. We witnessed 3-D movies and train wrecks at the MGM Studios. The children disappeared under six-foot waves at the man-made tidal wave pool in Typhoon Lagoon. We were carried by monorails, cable cars, steam trains, horse-drawn trolleys, but I think the best part of the Disney vacation was the parade.

Each night a spectacular parade of floats and people rolled down Main Street. All the people and all the floats were covered with strings of light. But it wasn't the parade itself, or the lights, but something that happened one evening that I will always remember.

We were sitting on the curb, watching the parade. Karen, my ten-year-old daughter, was waving to all the characters that went by: Snow White, Chip and Dale, Mickey Mouse, but no one waved back. Then another collection of characters began to dance by. They were young women dressed in beautiful butterfly costumes. Well, Karen waved and waved, then, suddenly, one of the butterfly dancers nearly flew over and stood right before Karen. My daughter looked up, and the butterfly stooped down and shook Karen's hand and asked, "Are you having fun?" in a beautiful Southern accent. Karen said yes, and the butterfly flew away down Main Street.

That simple little thing was one of Karen's favorites moments in Disney World: one person making her feel special.

It is so easy to see what God expects from us if we just look closely at the actions of people around us. "Make every effort to add to your faith goodness; and to goodness, knowledge; and to knowledge, self-control; and to self-control, perseverance; and to perseverance, godliness; and to godliness, brotherly kindness; and to brotherly kindness, love. For if you possess these qualities in increasing measure, they will keep you from being ineffective and unproductive in your knowledge of our Lord Jesus Christ" (2 Peter 1:5–8).

The kindness the young woman demonstrated toward my daughter at the parade that night would surely earn a compliment from the managers of the Disney corporation.

It is easy to reach out to a stranger and make him or her feel special. During the day, ask the postman, or the doctor, or the person in line in front of you if he or she is having a good day. It will make a bigger difference than you can imagine, and you will feel productive, effective, and you will earn a compliment from your day's manager: our Lord Jesus Christ.

Though I am humble, though I am small, though I am living my quiet life, I have power, Lord, to help others see. I have power, Lord, to help others smile. I have power, Lord, to be productive and effective in Your work. I share the news! I share the news! You have risen Lord, and we are loved.

Singing and Ducking Muck Balls

You who dwell in the dust, wake up and shout for joy.
ISAIAH 26:19

My parents moved to this country from Belgium in 1948, but all my relatives live across the ocean. One summer, when I was a teenager, my grandmother sent me airfare so that I might visit the family I never knew.

I was able to spend a few weeks with my aunt and uncle in southern France. During the first night of my visit, there was an extraordinary storm. The rain was heavy. Thunder and lightning fought all night between themselves, trying to see, it seemed, who had the most power.

The next morning I met my uncle at the breakfast table. "Your aunt is in the attic, cleaning up the mess. She won't let me help. See what you can do."

I walked up the attic stairs, and there I found my aunt scooping up dirt and muck from the floor. The roof had leaked the night before. Water had spilled into the old attic. My aunt was sopping up the filth and dropping it into a bucket. She was filthy. She looked horrible, and she was laughing and singing. I thought she was crazy.

"But, Christopher," she said. "I spent many years in a prison camp during the war. It was horrible. No work for me today is unpleasant. Come join me."

I spent the whole morning singing with my aunt. We threw muck balls at each other. We laughed. By lunchtime the attic was clean.

Did you ever have an experience that hurt you? We are not born to suffer. Difficult things happen to us all, but those things are not who we are. Faith in God lifts us beyond our sorrows. Each day we can say aloud to the Lord: "My comfort in my suffering is this: Your promise preserves my life" (Psalm 119:50).

We are meant to laugh and to sing. Try it. Join my aunt in the attic today and praise God.

Dear God, pour Your water on my suffering so my suffering turns to wine. Let me drink to You, my Lord. I make a toast to the promise. I bow down in Your presence. My pain is my garment. May we dance and shout in joy.

The Stability of God in Our Lives

Surely I have acted like a fool.

1 SAMUEL 26:21

One of the gifts I bought for my daughter's birthday was a volleyball set. I noticed a few days before her birthday that the children were playing their own version of the game, using a beach ball and the backyard fence as their net.

I drove to a sporting goods store and asked a salesman if he could help me pick out a good set.

We walked down an aisle filled with baseball bats, hockey sticks, lawn games, sneakers, until he pointed to a shelf with four types of volleyball equipment stored in boxes.

"Which one is the best?" I asked.

"Well, the ones with the thickest poles are good. Perhaps you'd like this set that also includes rackets for badminton. It's our most popular seller."

I bought the most popular seller, brought it home, wrapped it up, and placed it on the dining-room table along with the other presents for Karen's party.

The next day, after the cake, the songs, and the opening of presents, I sat on the back lawn with the open box, trying to understand the instructions for erecting the volleyball net.

A frustrating hour later, the net was up and the ball was inflated. The children played the rest of the afternoon, bouncing the ball over the net, then switching to the badminton rackets. It had been a good birthday.

I slept late the next morning and was awakened by the sound of laughter. I opened my shade and looked down in the yard, and there were the children, bouncing the beach ball back and forth over the backyard fence.

We have to be careful about what we want to improve in the world. Christ came to us to redirect our vision toward God in heaven and away from man-made gods: money, envy, power, faithlessness. Something ought not change: good memories, love, faith in the risen Lord.

If you are planning to make something better today, take a close look at what it is you want to do and ask yourself, "Is it really necessary?" Maybe we can take delight in celebrating the way things *are* instead of trying to make them into something that they ought not be.

As the air, as the soil, as the water abounds throughout the earth, so, too, Your presence, Lord, surrounds my life without fail. Is it possible, Lord, is it wonderfully possible that I could be so blessed in the continuity of Your divine love? I know the answer is yes, and yes I say to You, for in my answer to Your call I know I am secure.

Loving Your Neighbor

But a Samaritan, as he traveled, came where the man was; and when he saw him, he took pity on him. He went to him and bandaged his wounds.

LUKE 10:33–34

I was home alone with the children: five-year-old David, three-year-old Karen, and Michael, the infant. Roe was at work, her two-night-a-week position as a receptionist for an orthodontist. Just before dinner I realized that Karen had developed a high fever.

Perhaps I should take her to the doctor, I thought. Roe agreed, for I had called her at work for an opinion. After I hung up the phone, I walked out of the kitchen and found Karen slumped on the living-room couch. She was facing the ceiling and foaming at the mouth. Her eyes were rolled back. She was still and unconscious. I thought she was dying.

I didn't know what to do. Michael wasn't walking yet. David was bewildered. I simply wanted to run into the street and scream for help. I did scream: "Karen! Karen! Karen!" She wasn't responding.

The telephone. I called the police, the ambulance.

I rushed about through the dining room, through the living room, holding Karen, calling her name again and again, but there was still no response.

A minute later, I called the police again. "Please hurry!" Before I could place the receiver back in its place, the doorbell rang. Red and blue lights flashed throughout the neighborhood. I quickly answered the solid knocking, and there, standing before me, stood the tallest, broadest giant of a policeman I had ever seen. I could smell his leather coat. His shoes were shined. I wanted to hug him.

"I don't know what happened to my daughter! She isn't responding!"

"She's having a seizure," the policeman said in a low, confident voice. "Is she ill?"

"She has a fever! I know that! I was about to call the doctor!"

The policeman peacefully entered the house. "Let's take her upstairs and run some cool water in the bathtub. We need to bring her fever down a bit."

I pointed to the stairs. The policeman walked up, entered the bathroom, and began running the water. I was not aware that three or four neighbors had entered the house and were tending to David and Michael. I was not aware that the ambulance was on its way. All I knew was that a stranger was lifting my daughter out of my arms and gently placing her in a tepid tub of water.

I knelt on the floor to the left of the policeman. He, too, was kneeling and leaning over the wall of the bathtub, scooping up handfuls of water and slowly pouring them over Karen's hot back. His gun was belted to his waist. His badge scraped against the porcelain. As he was tending to Karen, he turned to me and whispered, "I have a three-year-old daughter, too."

Karen began to respond. I dried her with a towel, dropped it on the floor, and wrapped her in a wool blanket, and then I carried her downstairs. My neighbors said they would watch over the boys. The ambulance drove onto the front lawn and right up to the front door. Two-way radios squawked in the background.

After I again wrapped Karen in the blanket, after I stepped into the ambulance through that wide, rear door, after I sat down and held Karen against my chest, I cried and I cried.

The emergency room doctor said that Karen had suffered a febrile seizure, which some young children are prone to—a consultation with our family doctor was suggested. Her temperature dropped. Karen was fine.

In Tennessee Williams' play, *The Glass Menagerie,* Amanda, the mother, tells her son, "We have to do all that we can to build ourselves up. In these trying times we live in, all that we have to cling to is each other."

After my daughter was safely tucked in bed that night, as I walked past the bathroom I noticed that our policeman had drained the bathtub and folded the towels.

This policeman, my policeman had no reason to be so kind, so interested, so caring, but like the good Samaritan, he stopped his regular routine and felt compassion for me and for my daughter.

Jesus told the story about the Samaritan because He wanted to give an example of the type of people who will be rewarded eternal peace in heaven: those who love their neighbors for no reward.

Why don't you send several dollars in a friendship card today to someone you know who needs the money, but do not sign the card? It will be money in your pocket. Or volunteer your services at the local hospital once a week. It will be your best health care insurance. Give of yourself in the name of compassion, in the name of the Lord, and you will be rewarded.

Silence in my actions, silence in my love, creates a symphony for the Lord.

When Plans Succeed

Plans fail for lack of counsel, but with many advisers they succeed.
PROVERBS 15:22

I wanted to take the children to the circus. Better yet, I planned to take them to the greatest circus in the world in one of the greatest cities of the world: New York.

I bought the tickets, not realizing they were for the same day that Roe planned to take the children to the eye doctor, so she had to rearrange the schedule.

I waved the tickets above my head when I came home that night after I had made my purchase for ringside seats.

"The circus! We're going to the circus!" I announced.

"I don't want to go," my daughter quietly said.

"Why not?" I asked.

"Remember the last time? I'm afraid of the man on stilts."

"I'm not going," my older son said, "if I have to hear her complain the whole time."

Michael, the youngest, looked up and asked, "What's a circus?"

Three weeks later I was in the car, driving to New York with two children who had low fevers, one child who decided she wasn't going to open her eyes the whole time, and Roe who teased me saying, "Maybe we would have had a better time at the eye doctor's."

Have you ever stepped into a difficult situation because you didn't make plans? Do you even want to do something simply because you want to do it without asking anyone what they think?

We need advice. We need to explain our ideas to others before they are explained to the world. Christ selected His apostles to listen to His ideas about how the world ought to be. Well, those twelve listened, asked the Lord questions, and then they slowly understood what Christ was saying. I think Christ's plan succeeded, for He sought counsel, not only from His apostles but also from God.

If you are planning to do something today, ask yourself, "Did I ask those involved for ideas? Did I include others in my plan?"

And what about your eternal plans? Did you share your ideas with God today? Did you seek His counsel?

I need to plan the evening meal, plan my visit to the post office. I need to plan for the children's lunch, and their ride home from school. I need to plan my presentation at work. I need to plan for the next purchase order. My Lord God, as I prepare myself for the day, let me say that I also prepare myself for You, for I choose to succeed in Your eyes.

Is Anyone Home?

The LORD God said, "It is not good for the man to be alone."
GENESIS 2:18

After a long day at work, I was pleased to step out of the building. The car was cold. I brushed the freshly fallen snow from the windshield. It was dark, and I was tired.

As I drove along the streets, I looked out my window and thought about other people who were driving home at night in this same cold. Could other people feel as tired as I did? Could other people be looking at me through their car windows, wondering what I felt like?

I drove down the main street of my town, turned left, continued on my way through a yellow blinking light, made another left-hand turn, and pulled into my driveway.

I reached my briefcase from the backseat and dragged myself up the side stairs. The door was locked. I fished in my pocket, retrieved my set of keys, inserted the gray key into the lock, turned the key, and then I stepped into the house.

"Hi, everyone! I'm home!" The wind whipped the screen door against the railing outside. I reached out and closed the two doors.

"Hello!" I called out once again. Mittens, the cat, ran in from the living room and rubbed against my legs. I brushed her aside. She was shedding orange fur all over my new suit.

"Is anyone home?" I called out, just as I walked into the kitchen and found a note from Roe explaining that she and the children had driven to the mall and would be shopping and having dinner.

I opened the refrigerator door and rummaged around for dinner: a cold chicken leg, noodles, and a salad.

The house was silent. The rooms were empty. Again Mittens rubbed against me, and I was about to push her away again to protect my suit, but then she began to purr, so I leaned over and picked her up in my arms and began petting her under the chin. I broke off a piece of chicken and gave it to her. If she could, Mittens would have said "Thank you." She rubbed against my jacket, jumped off my lap, and ate the chicken with obvious delight.

After my lonely evening, Roe and the children finally returned. The back door burst open like a popped balloon. "Daddy! We're home," Michael yelled.

"Look at my new dress," Karen said, waving a bag above her head. David, my oldest son, rolled his eyes.

When Roe entered the house, she kissed me, then said, "Chris, your suit is a mess. It's covered with Mitten's hair."

"I know," I said. "It's nice in a way. Shows she's around. I missed you."

"Come, see Karen's dress," she answered, leading me by the hand toward the loud and full living room. Mittens cried to be let out. Her job was done.

Can you imagine how lonely Adam was without anyone there to keep him company? We are all alone in certain ways. Some of us live by ourselves, and others can be in a place full of people and still feel alone. But if we call out and say "I am lonely" someone will listen, especially God.

Tell a friend today, tell your husband or wife, tell your children that you are in need of their company, and they will come to you as the Lord comes to you each time you ask.

I am lonely, I am lonely, I am sometimes lonely, Lord, but I am never alone, for You are always in my heart and in my home. I am not afraid, because I seek Your companionship each day.

Protect What Is Small in God's Vast Kingdom

But ask the animals, and they will teach you, or the birds of the air, and they will tell you; or speak to the earth, and it will teach you, or let the fish of the sea inform you. Which of all these does not know that the hand of the LORD has done this?

JOB 12:7–9

I was ten years old and too young to understand the meaning of goals or perseverance. One night, just after I turned off my light, as my head pressed against my pillow, I thought I heard a noise—a distant sound, an animal sound, perhaps a scratching, then a small cry. Then I slept.

The next morning, while pulling on my socks, I heard again a slight scratching and a slight cry. Surely, there was something. I looked under my bed. Dust and comic books. I looked out my window. Maple tree. Wisteria vine.

Again, a slight scratching.

My room at the time, was on the third floor beside the attic. I walked up to the attic door and listened. Yes, a scratching. I pressed my ear against the door. Yes, a small cry. The light switch was under my fingertip. I opened the door. Trunks, old coats, a bookcase. Silence.

Just as I was about to return to my room, I heard, with more clarity, the same scratching sound and cry, a screeching sound perhaps.

The ceiling of the attic took the shape of the roof: high-peaked, slanting down toward the floor. I walked to my right, stepping over *National Geographic* magazines, past an old bathtub. The floor ended just at the edge where the roof ended. I found a large hole in the roof and a large pile of grass and twigs—an abandoned nest. Beyond the nest was the dark hole, the top of the wall space that ran down to the first floor.

Scratching. Crying. An empty nest. Perhaps? I ran back to my room, picked out a flashlight and a hand mirror from my box of treasures and ran back to the hole. Because the roof was angled down so close to the floor, I had to rest flat on my back, hold the mirror above my head, and aim the flashlight beam down the wall. There, in the reflection in the mirror, down the three-story space between the wall, I saw a bird, a young bird—a starling.

How many days had it been inside the wall? I quickly stood up and looked around the attic. I found a small, straw basket. I broke the sides of the basket, which created what I was looking for: a small, flat platform with a handle. I then tied a rope to the handle. I wiggled onto my back once again, adjusted the mirror, wedged the flashlight into the space so I didn't have to hold it. Then I slowly lowered my platform on a rope. Slowly, slowly, the small, broken basket wiggled closer and closer to the bird.

The room was hot. My back hurt. I realized I was under a spider-web. No one knew that a little boy was in the attic, trying to rescue a starling. I managed to lower the basket just within inches of the bird. Then I continued to drop it even lower until the platform rested right on the creature. What happened was what I had hoped would happen. Because there wasn't any space for it to escape, the bird started to shake, move, adjust its position as the basket pressed upon it until the platform was flat upon the bottom of the shaft, and the bird simply wiggled onto the platform for lack of any other place to sit.

Slowly, slowly, I began to pull the bird up and up. Slowly, slowly, until I reached down into the hole and held the bird in my hand. No magician could feel the same wonder I felt as I pulled the bird out of the darkness and held it up to the light. It squawked and kicked and squawked some more. It was too young to fly but old enough to be fed bits of meat and water, which it accepted eagerly.

My parents were proud of me when I told them what I had done. My sisters and brothers didn't believe me and thought I just took the bird from the nest.

Two months later, I opened my bedroom window. The starling, plump, full of feathers and energy, sat on my extended finger. I pushed my hand out the window. The bird held fast. I shook my hand a bit. The bird wobbled, flapped its wings vigorously, fell forward, extended those wings, quickly looped upward, and flew into the maple tree.

I leaned my arms against the windowsill. Then I placed my chin on my arms and looked at my starling. It twisted its head back and forth, and wiped its beak against the tree branch.

I liked what I had done.

If, as the Bible says that "in God's hands is the life of every creature and the breath of all mankind" (Job 12:10), it seems to make sense for a person to tend to an injured bird.

This might seem like an odd suggestion, but see if you can find a small creature that needs your assistance today: a trapped fly in the office, a worm washed up on the sidewalk, a ladybug stuck inside your kitchen window. Catch the fly and release it. Carry the worm back to the soil. Open the kitchen window and flick the ladybug back into the yard. If we pay attention to these small creatures, we will know the Creator a bit better. They might speak to us, tell us, teach us that, indeed, the Lord has done this.

Bless the fish and sea creatures; bless the sparrows. Bless my life and soul, Lord of the sheep and the lions, God of the great tigers and the small insects. God, bless all living things. Amen.

Slow to Speak, Slow to Anger

A hot-tempered man stirs up dissension, but a patient man calms a quarrel.

PROVERBS 15:18

One hot morning I was sitting on the deck, reading the newspaper, when I heard a loud, irritating, whirring noise. I turned the page of the paper, expecting the noise to stop after a while.

By the time I finished the last page of the newspaper, the irritating noise still cluttered the peaceful neighborhood.

I stood up from my chair and stepped around the corner of the house. The noise increased in volume. I looked to my left. Nothing. I looked to my right. Nothing. I looked up, and there it was—a fan, an attic fan in my neighbor's house—whirring, clanking, making a terrible, city-like racket.

My neighbor had installed the fan the day before. I was angry. *How can anyone disturb the peace with such a machine?* I asked myself. *And couldn't he have installed it on the opposite side of his house?*

For days I stomped around the house, complaining to my wife about this noise, this fan, this inconvenient, irritating nuisance.

Finally, after a week, I was fed up. I walked over to my neighbor's house, and rang the doorbell. My defense was prepared. My anger was controlled. I was going to ask him to disconnect that fan.

"Hi, Chris," my neighbor warmly greeted me. "Come on in."

"How are you, Jerry," I said as we shook hands.

"Well, better," he said. "We've had a bit of a scare the last few weeks. Anna [Jerry's daughter] developed a terrible breathing problem.. The doctor suggested fresh air, not air-conditioning, at night so I installed an attic fan. Anna finally sleeps at night again, so all is okay again."

Jerry looked at me. I looked at him, then he asked, "What's new with you?"

"Well," I said, "I, uh, was wondering if I could borrow your hedge clippers."

When I returned to my house, I clipped the bushes, swept the driveway, drove to town, bought the newspaper, and sat on my deck for the rest of the afternoon.

The noisy fan has never bothered me since.

"My dear brothers, take note of this: Everyone should be quick to listen, slow to speak and slow to become angry, for man's anger does not bring about the righteous life that God desires" (James 1:19–20).

If you are angry with someone, try to figure out today what is the cause of your anger. And try to discover why that person does what he or she does that angers you so.

If you take the energy you use to be angry and use it to work toward peace, there will be peace.

May the Lord be with me in my relationships with those that I know and meet. May the Lord help me see what He sees in us all: goodness, beauty, innocence. May the Lord grant me tolerance. For these things I pray.

Thanks in Everything

I will give you a wise and discerning heart.
1 KINGS 3:12

One morning in autumn my mother called me to her sewing room. I was a little boy full of energy and rough ways: I liked to chase my sisters with mud balls at that time.

"Christopher, I just finished knitting you this sweater. Let's try it on."

I remember that I wore a checkered shirt. The sweater was red and gray, a sleeveless vest with buttons in the front.

As my mother slipped the sweater on, I looked over her shoulder and made a funny face in the mirror behind her. My sisters called me "Dopey" when I was a child because of my huge ears. My ears stuck out, especially with the type of haircut from the late 1950s. My baby-sitter said that my ears were so big because my older brother pulled on them so often.

I was the type of child who didn't take big ears so seriously. (I secretly imagined that if I could flap them hard enough, I could fly like Dumbo.)

"Now," my mother said as she adjusted the sweater. "Look at yourself."

I stood before her mirror and looked like Dopey with a baggy sweater. It looked awful, but my mother had made it so I loved it.

Later in the afternoon, when I was in the yard, jumping into the pile of leaves my father collected, I noticed something. My buttons from the sweater had faces. Each button had two eyes, a nose, and a smile.

I ran into the kitchen and showed my mother the wonderful buttons. She embraced me. I wondered why.

Of course, I now understand why a mother would embrace a child who took free delight in something she did. I know with certitude my mother taught me to be grateful for what I have.

Are you grateful for all your blessings? Today rise up, "sing and make music in your heart to the Lord, always giving thanks to God the Father for everything" (Ephesians 5:19–20). Perhaps as a gesture of gratitude, you can make a gift for someone you love and add a secret extra something, like buttons with smiles.

I am grateful, Lord, I am grateful, Father. I am grateful, my God, for all that I am, for all that I do and see, for all that is possible. I am grateful to You for everything. Thank You and thank You. I bow my head and say, thank You. Amen.

It Was Very Good

A man will leave his father and mother and be united to his wife, and they will become one flesh.

GENESIS 2:24

As I walked to town for the Saturday newspaper, I found a wedding ring on the side of the road. Roe and the children were still sleeping. I was awake and anxious. The spring season had just exploded. The earth smelled rich and moist. The flowers were in bloom.

There is a stillness in a spring morning. The sky retains a soft blue. The sun is at the beginning of its full strength.

I like the silence at such times. I like the sense of loneliness. No man or woman lives without loneliness. Even among those we love we discover there is still a place in the heart that is not satisfied. Perhaps this feeling of emptiness is what makes someone write a book or sing a song. We make attempts each day to fill in the empty places in our hearts.

Halfway to the newspaper store, I saw a bit of color in the dirt. I leaned over and picked up a gold ring, a wedding ring.

I can imagine what it is like for an archaeologist to discover a bowl or an earring or an ancient tool deep inside a ceremonial cave. I can imagine the scientist trying to figure out what these artifacts mean, who owned them, what was their purpose.

The ring I found belonged to a woman. It was thin and small. Engraved on the inside were two names: Harry and Eve.

Did Eve toss the ring out of Harry's car? Did Harry anger Eve? Did Eve accept defeat in the relationship? Did Harry toss the ring out the window? Did Eve anger Harry? Did Harry accept defeat in the relationship?

I rolled the ring in my palm a few times, then I stuck it in my pocket and continued on my way.

By the time I arrived at the newspaper store, I had forgotten about the ring. I picked up the newspaper from the stacks, paid my money, and walked out of the store.

As I quickly scanned the headlines, I heard a crazy cry from the distant lake. There, in the middle of the water, I saw two small black dots. I walked a bit closer to the lake when the foolish cry began again; then one of the black dots turned into a pair of wings flapping over the water's surface.

Loons! Two loons!

I folded the newspaper under my arm and walked to the edge of the lake and sat on a bench. I watched the two birds swim together. At times they disappeared under the water and reappeared moments later. Again one of the birds gave out its loud cry. Was it a cry of love? A cry of anger? A cry in welcome to the new spring? I cupped my hands around my mouth and called out, "Hello, Harry! Hello, Eve!" The loons paid no attention.

By the time I returned from my walk, Roe was downstairs in the kitchen. The children were still sleeping.

"What's new?" she asked, as she often does when I return home with the newspaper. I walked up alongside her, gave her a kiss, then I said, "Nothing much. Just a pair of loons waking up together down on the lake."

How sad to think that two people lost a ring—that perhaps two people had lost their love for each other.

Love binds. It is what God wants for us. We leave our childhood and our parents so that we can strike out into a new journey, with a wife or husband. We live with loneliness, but "God created man in his own image, in the image of God he created him; male and female he created them" (Genesis 1:27). We find solace in the embrace of those we love. God made us. He understood our need for love. He created us for love. "God saw all that he had made, and it was very good" (Genesis 1:31).

I sent the ring to the police station, thinking that perhaps someone might return to look for it. No one did.

A policeman drove to the house one afternoon and returned the ring. "Sad, isn't it?" he asked. "Someone losing their wedding ring?"

Yes, I agreed, as I heard the children in the house, playing with the dog, and Roe talking in the background on the phone with her friend Linda.

In the end we always return to those we love. Embrace your husband or wife this evening. Call up a mother and father and wish them a good-night. And, in the end, there is always God. You are never alone. And that is very good.

In the union of marriage, there is God. In the union of life and death, there is God. In the union of parents and their children, there is God. In the union between friends, there is God. Thank You, Lord Jesus, for Your Word. "I will give you the keys of the kingdom of heaven; whatever you bind on earth will be bound in heaven" (Matt.16:19). Thank You, God, for the keys to Your heart. In this I pray. Amen.

A Child Is Born

Let's go to Bethlehem.

LUKE 2:15

Each December in the days when I was young, the congregation of the Presbyterian church down the road built a manger, spread real straw on the floor, and arranged in the new construction life-size figures of the Holy Family, two sheep, a donkey, shepherds, and three kings. It was part of our family's tradition in the Christmas season to visit this crèche.

Early one December when I was nine years old, my father announced that we were going to walk downtown and pay our respects to the baby Jesus. This visit was unique because we walked to the church after dark. In the past we had always driven to the manger scene because it was too cold to walk, and there was always a baby in our family that prevented us from pursuing much adventure. When I was nine, the baby was four, could walk on her own, and wanted to carry the flashlight.

"Everyone—take a hat and gloves. It's very cold," my mother announced as she reached into the closet for our coats.

We walked out of the house and proceeded to follow my four-year-old sister in single file down the sidewalk. Now that I look back it was like following a star, in a way, the star of Bethlehem in the hands of my little sister leading us to the newborn King.

By the time we arrived at the manger, my father was carrying my sister in his arms and the flashlight batteries had died, but the church had erected soft lights that illuminated the ancient scene that stood before us. My mother reminded us that we celebrate Christmas as a reminder of Christ's birthday. She retold the story of Mary and Joseph, how they were searching for a vacant inn. While my mother spoke about the manger, I leaned over and touched the robe of one of the three kings. To my surprise, a small yellow piece of the robe broke off and fell into my hand. I didn't know what to do with it. I didn't want to tell my parents because I was afraid that they might be angry that I had ripped the robe of one of the three kings. I didn't want to drop the piece of cloth because I felt it was sacrilegious, like dropping the American flag to the ground, so I quickly stuck the yellow bit of cloth into my pocket just as my mother finished telling us about the angels and the arrival of the three kings.

"Time to go home," my father announced as he rearranged my sleeping sister on his shoulder.

That night my sisters and brothers, my mother and father, and I walked home in the dark. As we entered the house, my father flicked on a single lamp in the living room so that we could find our way upstairs and to our beds.

After brushing our teeth, after slipping into our pajamas, and after kissing my parents good-night, I pulled the yellow piece of cloth out of my pants pocket and slipped it under my pillow.

Three wise men also followed a light many years ago. What they found at the end of their journey was a Child who filled them with immense joy. They kneeled down before the Child. Perhaps they smiled, nodded their heads in approval, praised Mary and Joseph. These three kings stepped back and unwrapped the gifts they brought: gold, frankincense, and myrrh. This is what my mother told me.

I kept the yellow piece of cloth from the robe of the wise man for many years. Perhaps it was a gift. I believed for a time that the cloth had magical powers, perhaps the power to keep my hands warm, or the power to illuminate a dark room.

Today I understand the true gift of the Magi: the Christmas faith, the image of Mary and Joseph protecting the Baby, my father carrying my sister home on his back.

We all have bits of the wise man's cloth in our hands. It is our responsibility to use this gift, to believe in its power, to be humble in the reality that something significant happened a little over two thousand years ago in the small town of Bethlehem. It is our faith. It is our salvation.

"I bring you good news of great joy that will be for all the people," the angels said to the shepherds. "Today in the town of David a Savior has been born to you; he is Christ the Lord" (Luke 2:10–11).

Today, and every day, enjoy the simple wonders of the Lord. Glory to God in the highest, and peace on earth and goodwill to all. Today let's go to Bethlehem.

Glory to God, and glory to God. In thanks for the Good News for all time and for all people, let us raise our hands in glory, great glory to God.

Epilogue

"Finally, brothers [and sisters], whatever is true, whatever is noble,whatever is right, whatever is pure, whatever is lovely, whatever is admirable—if anything is excellent or praiseworthy—think about such things. Whatever you have learned or received or heard from me, or seen in me—put it into practice. And the God of peace will be with you" (Philippians 4:8–9).